FROM **TRAGEDY** TO **TRIUMPH**

LIFE AFTER LOSS

WANDA JOHNSON

Published by TragedyTruimph Publishing
Hayward, CA 94545

© 2024 Wanda Johnson

Interior Book Design & Formatting: Tywebbin Creations

Editor: Paulette Nunlee, Five Star Proofing

Book Coach: Dr. Paulette Harper www.pauletteharper.com

All rights reserved. No part of this book may be used or reproduced, stored in or introduced into a retrieval system, or transmitted in any form, including photocopying, electronic or mechanical, recording, or by any means without the express written consent from the author.

Scripture quotations marked "KJV" are taken from the Holy Bible, King James Version, Cambridge, 1769. Used by permission.

Scriptures marked CEV are taken from the CONTEMPORARY ENGLISH VERSION. Copyright© 1995 by the American Bible Society. Used by permission.

Library of Congress Cataloging-in-Publication Data

Paperback: ISBN: 979-8-218-36243-0

Published and printed in the United States of America.

Contents

Praise for Wanda Johnson From Tragedy To Triumph	VI
Disclaimer	XI
Dedication	XIII
In Loving Memory	XV
Acknowledgments	XVII
Foreword Areva Martin, Esq.	XXI
Chapter 1 Tragedy	1
Chapter 2 Life Without a Father	3
Chapter 3 Walking the Road You Make	11
Chapter 4 A Good Name	17

Chapter 5 The Last Celebration	21
Chapter 6 A Phone Call You Never Want to Receive	27
Chapter 7 The Last Turn of Fate	35
Chapter 8 A Story Worthy of Reporting	41
Chapter 9 It's So Hard to Say Goodbye	45
Chapter 10 Picking Up The Pieces	55
Chapter 11 Falling Into A Hole	61
Chapter 12 Walking In Purpose	67
Chapter 13 Community Rally Cry For Justice	73
Chapter 14 Change of Venue	81
Chapter 15 Demanding Justice	87

Chapter 16 A Fourteen Year Sentence	95
Chapter 17 Money Can Separate Families	101
Chapter 18 Keeping Oscar's Legacy Alive	105
Chapter 19 The Movie: Fruitvale Station	115
Chapter 20 A Road of Ministry	119
Chapter 21 Come On and Fight For Your Child	123
Chapter 22 God Has Not Forgotten You	131
The Story of Rizpah	137
Wanda's Homemade New Year's Eve Gumbo	139
About the Author	143

Praise for Wanda Johnson
From Tragedy To Triumph

A masterpiece of love sewn delicately together with treasured memories of love, joy, and pain. Pastor Wanda Johnson threads the needle of our emotions to the insane story of a Mother's unbreakable love for her gifted son, stolen by the never-ending crime of social injustice. The supposedly secret internal hatred of a culture destined for greatness by God!

A love story woefully expressed by one person, representing an entire culture of broken-hearted parents combatting the constant war of the genocide of our children, men, and women.

Rev. Dr. Gloria Word
Author of *Casual Christianity and the Loss of Family Values*
Professor/Advisor/Project Director, Good News Seminary and Bible College

I've heard many people talk about how they turned their pain into purpose, Tragedy to Triumph, but never witnessed such a one like Reverend Wanda Johnson, the mother of the late Oscar Grant III. You might ask why I address her with the prefix of Reverend. I do it intentionally. It depicts her faith. Faith in her God allowed her the opportunity to turn her pain into purposeful living after Oscar's death.

After much questioning and many tears, she became a champion who fought for justice for her son. She quickly accepted the call to aid parents all over the world to do the same, as she witnessed them experience the heartbreak of losing a child. She is called Mother Wanda by her peers and rightfully so. She takes time to nurture those who grieve their losses.

She is the CEO of the Oscar Grant Foundation, a foundation that endeavors to aid disenfranchised and at-risk youth in achieving their dreams.

"Reverend" is an anglicization of the Latin reverendus, meaning "one who must be respected." As I witness her journey, she is truly a woman respected by her peers, community leaders, local and intergovernmental agencies, faith-based community and people from all walks of life.

Warm regards,
Saundra Eve-Jones

When Wanda Johnson's son Oscar Grant III was taken from her by the bullet of a BART police officer, she was devastated as she grieved his lost dreams—of raising his daughter, becoming a barber and becoming the man he was meant to be—and hers, of doing ministry with her son. The same grief that once took her breath away led Wanda to redefining her purpose. Although her son Oscar Grant III is not with her in physical form, his spirit lives on in Wanda Johnson's work as she supports mothers and families across the world who've lost children to police violence and works toward a world that is more equitable and just for everyone. *From Tragedy to Triumph* is a must read that has the capacity to restore hope in humanity, inspire action for change and lead readers to find the silver lining in life's darkest moments.

FROM TRAGEDY TO TRIUMPH

Sharon K. Sobotta
Writer & Journalist

Our country's most precious resource is being lost to violence right here upon our nation's soil.

I came to know this lovely and tight-knit family over five decades ago through Author Wanda Johnson's cousin, whom you meet in the first chapters of *From Tragedy To Triumph* as Oscar Grant III comes into the world.

As a woman who has not had children, I was still drawn into this very personal and poignant story. Wanda pulls you in and sits you down with her. She tells a compressed, yet surprisingly fully-detailed, narrative that not just embraces the abrupt cessation of Oscar's life, but brings us—the reader—into a world not tainted by the one-sided slant of television or news.

The picture of a life of what occurs before the pain, during the pain, after the pain, and even when the pain still remains. Wanda shows how, through God, family, friends, and perseverance—and yes, this is very cliché—she turned pain into purpose.

Dear reader, may you enjoy *From Tragedy To Triumph* as I have.

God Bless,

Velma Y. Harris

Disclaimer

This nonfiction book contains references to real individuals, living or deceased, and events based on historical or factual accounts. Every effort has been made to ensure the accuracy and integrity of the information presented within this book. Names of individuals have been used solely for the purpose of providing accurate and informative content.

It is important to note that any opinions, interpretations, or conclusions drawn in this book are the author's own and do not necessarily reflect the views or opinions of the individuals mentioned, their families, or any associated parties.

The author has made reasonable efforts to respect the privacy and rights of individuals referenced in this work. Any portrayal or representation of these individuals is based on available information and historical records.

Readers are encouraged to conduct further research and verification if they wish to delve deeper into the lives and experiences of the individuals mentioned in this book.

The author, not being an expert in foundation set-up, provides advice and information on the subject matter to the best of her knowledge and abilities. Readers should seek professional advice and consult experts when making decisions related to setting up a foundation or related activities.

While the author acknowledges the book coach's advice against including personal names in this work, she has decided to incorporate them nonetheless.

This decision absolves the book coach of any liability regarding the inclusion of personal names.

While every attempt has been made to ensure the reliability of the information, the author, and the book coach cannot be held responsible for any errors or discrepancies.

Dedication

From Tragedy to Triumph is dedicated to Oscar Grant III. It explores the fight for justice, love, and equality for those who have suffered at the hands of injustice. Your legacy will live on, and you will never be forgotten.

In Loving Memory of Oscar Juliuss Grant III

1986-2009

And he said, While the child was yet alive, I fasted and wept: for I said, Who can tell whether God will be gracious to me, that the child may live? But now he is dead, wherefore should I fast? Can I bring him back again? I shall go to him, but he shall not return to me.
II Samuel 12:22-23 (KJV)

Acknowledgments

I want to thank the following: God first because without him, I would probably be in a hospital somewhere. God, my father, gave me life and purpose. He turned my pain into purpose that I was blinded to at first. I thank God for giving his son Jesus as a live sacrifice who had done no wrong. I live, preach, and offer words of hope because of him. I've learned to bless him at all times.

Cedric Moore, my husband, whom I've known for over forty-six years. Thank you for your continued support, the encouraging words, and push to keep going and not give up. Thank you for giving me the space to take the time to write and finish this book. Thank you for the continuous push to grow in my gifts and calling. Through all the ups and downs, you have continued to support me behind the scenes.

I would also like to thank and express my love for my mother, who never gave up on me. She continually prayed and spoke over my life with words that would not let me forget who and what God has done in my life. Mother, I thank you. You have been a rock and a model of someone that loves God, and you walk it and show it. I love you.

To my daughter, Chantay: Thank you for the days I was down. You would say a word of encouragement and cause me to get up and start over again. On days when I did not feel I could complete the book, you and Leroy (grandson) would double-team me and say something positive when I wanted to operate in the negative. Thank you. I love you both.

To my brothers and sisters: Cephus Jr., Charmine Jones, Daryl Johnson, Kenneth Johnson. I would not have made it without you. Thank you for your support and love. You all sacrificed to ensure we got a measure of justice. I humbly thank and love you.

Special thanks go to Pastor Deborah Rodgers: you spoke into my life at a time when I was in great despair. Thank you for the prayers, anointing with oil, and the words you spoke over my life. I have seen them come to pass. Thank you so much.

To my sisters, Donna Smith and Saundra E. Jones: You took care of me when I could not take care of myself. Words cannot describe how it made me feel. You were there day and night when I called. Thank you so much.

To Palma Ceia Baptist Church and all the other churches and community members:

Thank you for praying for me and my family and for supporting and loving us. We appreciate and thank you for all you did.

To all the community: We thank you for standing with us, for praying for us and for traveling back and forth to court with us. We could have never done it without your support

Muhammad Mosque#26B: Thank you for allowing your fierce leader Minister Keith Muhammad the opportunity to support my family. We thank and appreciate you all. Thank you, Minister Keith, for all you did to ensure justice was served. Thank you for traveling with my family and never missing or leaving until the court sessions ended.

Sister Beatrice X Johnson, you drove me hundreds of miles, took care of me, sang, cried, and prayed with me. Thank you. There are so many community members who supported me during this difficult time. Without you, I would not have made it. Thank you so much for your love and support.

Foreword

Areva Martin, Esq.

The devastating killing of Oscar Grant III has been captured powerfully in the public realm. Now, more than a decade on, Wanda Johnson opens her broken heart to us with *From Tragedy to Triumph,* the story of a mother's unyielding grief.

Turning pain into purpose has always been a mainstay of Black existence. Black mothers, in particular, have demanded through their pain, that we pay attention to the losses of their children—and that we act. Time and again, generation after generation, they have forced us to reckon with the truth of what those reprehensible acts of violence say about a society. On January 1, 2009, Wanda Johnson joined a community of mothers bound by the ties of their children's horrific murders.

She captures and conveys the full picture of Oscar's loss by sharing not only his story, but her own. As excruciating as it is to walk alongside Wanda as she revisits Oscar's life, we should be honored that she permits us to bear witness. And we must refuse to give into the very human temptation to move on. In *From Tragedy to Triumph,* Author Wanda Johnson refuses to let America look away.

Chapter 1

Tragedy

The phone rang a little after 2:15 a.m.

I was sitting in the living room watching television with my husband.

The voice on the other end was crying and screaming. I could not understand what was being said.

Oscar's fiancée finally got the words out. "Oscar got shot!"

I said, "Oscar. My son? What happened?"

She said again, "Oscar was shot!"

I jumped up out of the chair, yelling, "Oscar got shot!"

It took a while for the words to sink in.

I screamed, "What happened?" I would repeat the question several times.

WANDA JOHNSON

It was a mother's worst nightmare.

Chapter 2

Life Without a Father

Lying on the tan shaggy carpeting in my mother's family room, my contractions were coming one on top of the other. I couldn't help screaming. I'd already been sent home earlier that day from the hospital. I needed to be sure I was truly ready to leave home again. A cousin was with me.

"Aunt Bonnie," she yelled. "Better hurry up, or Wanda's gonna have this baby on your floor."

When I caught my breath from the pain, I went straight into a belly laugh. "Girl, are you having this baby, or am I?" The next contraction kicked in and shut me right up.

"Like it or not, we're going!" my mother said, rushing in from the kitchen.

Six hours later, Oscar Grant III came into the world kicking and screaming, weighing in at seven pounds, six ounces, and twenty-one inches long.

At four months, he was already drinking collard greens juice. He was a fast learner all his life, taking his first steps to walk at seven months old.

We lived in Oakland for the first four years of his life, then moved to Hayward with my parents and later resided in San Leandro, California. Because of his father's incarceration, Little Oscar never lived in the same house as his father. It was sad; I never dreamed that for my child. I grew up looking at the fairy tale marriage my parents had. I thought of my family as upper-class, where both parents worked. My children were being raised by a single parent. However, my father and brothers, along with men in the church, provided a male influence.

Oscar III was introduced to his father for the first time at four months old. At five years old, he started to remember who his father was. I took Oscar, his great-great-grandmother, and Chantay, his sister, to Old Folsom State Prison several times to see him. On Saturdays, we would leave home around six in the morning. I would fill the car with gas and buy a few snacks to eat on the way for the two-and-a-half-hour drive. Once we arrived, we waited in line to check in. We had to have the right clothes. The right colors. The line was sometimes lengthy, so it was essential to be timely for set check-in times. At our turn, I had to show my identification and Oscar's and Chantay's birth certificates. I was allowed twenty dollars in quarters to buy food there. After the check-in, we had to wait outside for a bus to drive us to the inmate's housing unit.

Prison was such a sad place. Visiting time was limited, and you couldn't touch the inmate. I will never forget the metallic clanging of the prison bars closing behind us.

It was tough to explain to Oscar why his father was in prison. Embarrassed at first—and maybe ashamed—I was with someone who was locked up. I couldn't share with anyone that we went to see my son's father at Folsom Prison on some weekends. I knew my son was saddened because he played baseball, and all his teammates had both parents at the team's games. He longed to see a father of his own there, sometimes calling Chantay's father "Dad."

Oscar attended parochial and public schools. He truly enjoyed his first: Lea's Christian School, a K-4 private school. A fast-paced school, he liked math and reading, mastering multiplication in the first grade.

I would drop him off in the morning and act as a yard duty teacher until 9:30 a.m. Once a month, I'd deliver the chapel message for the school.

During his years at Lea's, Oscar was introduced to sports. Soccer at recess, and after school he would play kickball. For whatever reason, Oscar enjoyed the outdoors and playing with balls.

He got a kick out of being in the spotlight, so he volunteered when there was an opportunity to be seen as a leader. At six, he learned to play chess during the after-school program. He became a skilled player; he often challenged his uncles and cousins for hours. Although he tried to teach me, I never understood the concept. His triumphant shout of "checkmate" made me smile.

After graduating fourth grade, he attended Community Christian School (CCS) in San Leandro. A different curriculum than Lea's, but the same size student-wise, with less than 200 enrollees.

He liked CCS, and I encouraged his participation in sports. He enjoyed playing soccer there and played with one of the female students, who'd later become a friend for life. A very spirited competitor, he hated losing, pouring all his energy into whatever he did.

He ventured into playing baseball, football, and basketball. One year, I signed him up late for baseball. Unfortunately, he had to settle with a spot playing on the younger team, the Pirates. He was soon hitting home runs each time he went up to bat. His teammates adored him and looked up to him. Oscar reveled in all the attention he received; he felt like a superstar. The Pirates believed they would win the championship with Oscar on their team. The opposing teams' pitchers tossed unreachable balls to Oscar, trying to walk him automatically when he came to the plate. Some of our team's parents complained it was unfair. Parents on the other teams argued it wasn't fair because he was too old and too big. The league manager disagreed with both sides. He ruled Oscar would continue to play for the Pirates, and the opposing pitchers should pitch to him the same as to the other players.

I recall when the family traveled to Los Angeles to a cousin's house, a *fearless* Oscar jumped into the ten-feet-deep end of the swimming pool. Never taking one swimming lesson, I couldn't believe my eyes. It all happened quickly. My dad just jumped in, clothes, shoes, and wallet on him. It didn't matter. He would save his grandson. My father emerged from underwater with Oscar in his arms. Once they reached the surface, Oscar laughed. Scared, I was nervous and holding my breath the whole time. But Oscar thought it was funny.

Oscar started his eighth-grade junior high year at Bohannon Middle School in San Lorenzo. At first, it was difficult; he'd been used to a different structure. His day had started with prayer, then going to chapel for worship services—students singing, dancing, and listening to a message by the assigned pastor. The first few months, he would report he missed chapel and his old school friends. I visited the school several times monthly to check his grades and behavior. He had so much energy.

A teacher shared a story about his class experiment. He hadn't given up his determination to stand out. Oscar stuck a pencil in his hair to see if it would stay. He was wearing an afro at the time. The teacher thought it was hilarious. With the pencil in his hair, he tried to play basketball with one hand while holding his pants up with the other.

His eighth-grade graduation at Bohannon Middle School was memorable. Dressed in a white suit and black Stacey Adams shoes, he was excited and proud of how nice he looked. When his name was called, he strutted to the stage like he owned the world. He climbed the stairs and raised both arms. Confidently, he accepted his diploma. Facing the audience with a beaming smile, he waved his certificate of completion. I was grateful he'd passed one hurdle.

Chapter 3

Walking the Road You Make

Oscar played football during his first year at San Lorenzo High School. Once, he got hurt during the game and was rushed to the hospital. His injury wasn't serious; eight hours later, he was released. He tried almost every sport. Having asthma made it difficult for him to breathe at times. But that didn't deter him. It seemed odd because he could play football and basketball and only experienced asthma attacks when playing baseball.

I remember one attack, the inhaler filled with Albuterol wasn't working. I drove him the two blocks to St. Rose Hospital. When I raced into the emergency room with him in my arms, nurses could see he was having an asthma attack and immediately took him into a bay. He wasn't breathing. I was in tears. They placed the oxygen mask over his mouth and nose and injected a shot. They sent me out to wait. Scared and nervous, there was nothing I could do but pray. I prayed, and I cried. Once stabilized, he was released. Back home, Oscar got stronger and stronger. By the third day, he was back to normal. Teasing his sister and anxious to return to school.

Oscar bugged me to transfer him to Mount Eden High School. I feared he would become distracted because he knew more people there than at San Lorenzo. I avoided the transfer for six months. He was so persistent, nagging, and begging. Finally, I gave in and transferred him.

His behavior and attitude toward school soon changed. It was one of the worst decisions I made as a parent regarding his education. Oscar made it through the ninth grade with declining grades. I wasn't sure if it was because he began working at fourteen at KFC or was just bored with school. For whatever reason, Oscar began cutting school. He remained on the basketball team with plummeting grades. In a conference with his teachers, they offered to tell me how smart he was. Even sharing his test scores—surprisingly high A's and B's. I warned him about skipping classes. He was bored and I suspected there was more to his actions.

While still making passing grades, his interest in school was tanking fast. I continued to talk to him about his poor attendance. After a while, he started doing better again. Like a cycle, he would attend school and bring his grades up. Then, his steps would falter and after a few months, his attendance tumbled again. He kept his grades at the required level so he could play basketball and continue working. He would do the very minimum. From his behavior, his scholar days were over. You could tell he no longer wanted to attend school.

By this time, a turn for the worst was occurring. He would miss weeks of school, sneaking off with his girlfriend and friends. He started smoking weed, and your guess is as good as mine as to what else. The weed's scent was so strong that when I washed his clothes, I would find bottles of Old Spice and Visine in his pockets. I guess he thought I wouldn't know, if he had clear eyes and strong cologne distracted the smell.

I tried to steer him back in the right direction. The more I prayed, went to his school and where he hung out, the worse things unraveled. I regretted the decision to transfer him to a school where his friends attended. I wouldn't dare say his behavior changed because of a different school or hanging with his friends. Although, the move helped change the course of his life.

I'd tried bribing him, tired of begging him to attend class. There were days I'd drop Oscar off at the front door, and by the time I drove off, he'd be walking out the school's back door. I'd leave work to look for him, worrying myself sick. Friends advised me to put him out, and he wasn't even eighteen years old. I didn't think it was wise for me to give up on him.

After about a year, he finally quit school, but wanted to continue working. I was disappointed because his sister had already graduated from Mount Eden High School and worked full-time. Oscar was a complete dropout, still trying to work part-time. I had these goals and expectations for my son, and he'd failed them all, so I thought.

Spiraling out of control, he stayed out late at night. His excuse was not having a father at home; he needed a dad who was a part of his life. Maybe by guilt-tripping me, he thought he could get his way. It was a bumpy road for about four years.

FROM TRAGEDY TO TRIUMPH

Chapter 4

A Good Name

Oscar always managed to keep a job, beginning his first job at fourteen. I suspect money contributed to the reason he dropped out of school. Once he was making money each week, he didn't see the need for an education. While working at KFC—and not completely dropped out of school—his fiancée found out she was pregnant.

Although Oscar was excited about the pregnancy, he didn't want to be the father boarding the bus with his baby in a stroller. So, he saved his money to purchase a means of transportation. While searching, he came across a pastor who was selling a car. The seller lived in Hayward and allowed Oscar to set up a weekly payment arrangement to purchase his car. After the final payment, he received the keys. Excited about being a first-time car owner and soon-to-be father, he hung pink flags that read *It's a Girl* in his new car.

He drove down the street with the flags waving. The baby arrived, and he loved her to pieces. He had a job, a car, and now a newborn baby, and Oscar still struggled.

He ended up getting into trouble with the law and going to jail for six months—then, went back again. There was nothing I could do except pray for him. I visited him and reminded him of a scripture from the Bible I'd told him about often: Proverbs 22:1 (KJV). A good name is more desirable than great riches and loving favour rather than silver and gold. All he had was his name. Things would get hard for him once he messed up his name. It would be hard to find a job and for people to trust him. Also to secure more education and housing.

He applied to take the GED test and passed. With the certificate in hand, he tried to get his life on track again. He sent me a list of his twenty-one goals. I remember reading the goals that included: a place for his family in Livermore, continue being a butcher working in a meat department, barber cosmetology school. All I could do was pray he would achieve those goals.

It was very disappointing as a parent; I thought I had failed. I thought he'd failed because he dropped out of school.

Every parent goes through something with their child—whether good or bad. I always think and smile about the twenty-one goals Oscar hoped to obtain but never got a chance to fulfill. Part of parenthood is being able to endure when tested. I was reminded when Oscar was struggling that he was my sheep. Just as I am God's sheep, and He continues to care for me, I should be willing to do the same for my child. No matter how tough the struggle, as parents, it's our job to love our children.

Bishop T. D. Jakes once spoke that he loves his children no matter what. I took on the same mindset: I vowed to love Oscar through the good and through the bad. Not supporting the bad, but praying for God to deliver and set him free.

If this reminds you of your child, do not give up on them. Don't throw them away. Keep praying, believing God for your child, believing that God can change them. What the enemy means for evil, God can turn it around for good. I always held on to that scripture. God can deliver anyone he chooses. Let your child know you love them during the good and the bad. Too often we throw away our children too fast. I vowed to love Oscar the way Christ loves his church. To love him no matter what. I may not like it, but I loved him.

Oscar was maturing and beginning to see the importance of life. We all have to grow up, and he was on his way to transformation.

Chapter 5

The Last Celebration

Oscar was working at Oakland Farmer Joe's, training to become a butcher. He loved working because he wanted money for the holidays. He enjoyed the holidays and celebrated Thanksgiving and Christmas 2008 with family and friends. He had my birthday off—December 31—and we planned on celebrating together.

I received my first phone call at 8 a.m. before I had my morning devotion. The call wasn't before sunrise, but it was way too early. I was still asleep.

Oscar's first words were, "Happy birthday, Mother."

Then, his fiancée, Sophina and daughter, Titiana, said, "Happy birthday." My granddaughter sang Happy Birthday to me, her four-year-old voice so loud you could hear it all over the house.

Oscar said, "I will be over later today to spend the day with you." He wanted to know my plans for the day. We'd meet at my parents' house. He said, "I love you and will see you later." As usual, the younger brother wanted to be the oldest, so Oscar called his sister to remind her to call her mother.

So, whatever he said worked, because Chantay and my grandson, Leroy, called next, singing Happy Birthday. She asked what I wanted.

I, jokingly, said, "I want a million dollars. Can you bring it to me?" We all laughed about spending the money and ended the call. I couldn't believe it was New Year's Eve and she wouldn't be celebrating with us because she had to work. After all, after fifteen years, Chantay was the manager at KFC.

A few hours later, dressed in the new red outfit I'd purchased, with hair and makeup done, I was excited about the day. I couldn't stop talking about it. I loved birthday celebrations as much as Oscar loved bearing gifts. I anticipated a festival where I would receive cards with money and gifts.

I greeted my mother and then went into my father's room and visited him. My father was home, almost bedridden. His health had declined from an earlier stroke.

It was time to cook gumbo. It was a tradition for my family every year. Oscar loved my gumbo, and he would eat at least two or three bowls.

Finally, the food was ready. The house smelled good. I dished out bowls of gumbo for Oscar, his fiancée, my granddaughter, and myself. We ate and joked. My granddaughter gave me a birthday card. I was so excited that I opened the card, and a dollar fell to the floor. Oscar asked for another bowl of gumbo and couldn't eat it all. So, he started spooning his gumbo into my bowl when my back was turned.

I was such a proud mother as I celebrated my birthday, and the end of a challenging year. I anticipated the new year would be filled with blessings as Oscar began a fresh chapter of his life, getting another opportunity to make better decisions. Another opportunity to join his fiancée and his four-year-old daughter.

He had visions of helping support and sustain his family as a barber. I had dreams and plans for Oscar's life. Sometimes, as parents, we make all these goals and dreams for our children, and they have plans for their lives. We want our children to fulfill our goals, and our children have their own. I also had peace because I remembered what the Lord had shown me concerning him.

Oscar said he was going to San Francisco. His daughter cried, not wanting her daddy to leave her that evening. Oscar gave her a dollar and promised to take her to Chuck E. Cheese the next day.

He stayed at my birthday celebration gathering until just over an hour before he'd meet up with friends to travel to San Francisco. They'd watch the fireworks show and the new year come in. He took my words to heart that night.

"Don't drive," I said, kissing him goodnight. "I don't want you drinking, driving, or getting into trouble by getting pulled over. Take the BART and be safe."

The sendoff was short and sweet. Oscar had to drop off their daughter at his fiancée's aunt's house before going to San Francisco.

After all, I knew Oscar and I would be together again in a few hours. As he walked out the door that night, I began to thank the Lord. It would be a good year full of fresh starts, new beginnings, and better choices. I could feel it in every fiber of my being. I thought about taking a picture of all of us and praying with them before they left. I put off the very things I had an opportunity to do. I knew what God had shown me was about to come to pass. We would be together, so I vowed to take pictures and pray with them on New Year's Day.

I truly wish my granddaughter had not accepted the dollar bribe. I wish she had held him so tight and not let him go. That he had heard her cry and changed his mind. I wished I could turn back time and start the day again.

Chapter 6

A Phone Call You Never Want to Receive

The time was getting closer to midnight, and I reminisced about the fun day. Had I known what was really to come that night, my life, Oscar's life, the life of his daughter, his fiancée, his uncles and aunts, his sister, cousins, and friends might have been different or simpler.

The phone rang a little after 2:15 a.m.

I was sitting in the living room watching television with my husband.

The voice on the other end was crying and screaming. I could not understand what was being said.

Oscar's fiancée finally got the words out. "Oscar got shot!"

I said, "Oscar. My son? What happened?"

She said again, "Oscar was shot!"

I jumped up out of the chair, yelling, "Oscar got shot!"

It took a while for the words to sink in.

I screamed, "What happened?" I would repeat the question several times.

I jumped up out of the chair, yelling, "Oscar got shot!" It took a while for the words to sink in. I repeated the question several times.

My husband and Oscar had just been together earlier at Chantay's house. He shouted, "Oscar got shot."

We immediately ran out the apartment door to the car. I don't remember anything. Did I pick up my purse and turn off the television or lights? Or even if I locked the door. I ran down the stairs, opened the passenger door, and sat in the front seat crying. Cedric jumped in the driver's seat and drove down the street, turning onto the freeway. He sped north on 880 at over 100 miles an hour. Watching the speedometer numbers rise, I wasn't worried about being stopped by the police.

My adrenaline was high, and my heart was pumping so fast. All I could do was pray and ask God to let Oscar be okay.

Our first stop was at the Fruitvale BART Station to collect Oscar's fiancée and friends. Then, the drive to the Highland Hospital in Oakland where the ambulance was taking Oscar. It seemed like an eternity to get there.

While on the way there, I asked them again what happened. They repeatedly said, "Oscar did not do anything." I wondered about so many things. If he was trying to run. Was he resisting arrest? Was he drunk in public? Did he have a gun? Did he try to fight the police? *What happened?* All the negative things that could have caused the shooting entered my mind.

I talked to God. I kept saying, "Oh, Jesus, oh God, please, Lord, help him. Help me, Lord, touch him.

"Jesus, touch him. Lord, touch him."

I began to plead the blood of Jesus. The anxiety was indescribable, and my body was shaking all over. The tears would not stop flowing down my face. My faith in God had turned to fear of the unknown. I quoted 2 Timothy 1:7 (KJV), "For God hath not given us a spirit of fear; but of power and of love and of a sound mind." All kinds of thoughts were going through my mind.

We finally arrived at the hospital. His friends, the ones who had gone on to the hospital, reported what happened:

Oscar and his friends were on their way back from San Francisco, and a call was placed to the train operator that there was pushing and shoving on the train. The police came, responding to reports of a fight on the train. The train was crowded because it was New Year's.

The officer who arrived focused on black males, and Oscar was one of the ones singled out and held. The officer did not see anything going on, but per the witnesses, appeared mad and aggressive. He came on the platform, cursing and yelling. He told some of the young men to "get the F#!* off the train." He was using racial epithets, yelling, and ordering the young men off the train and to stand against the wall. The officer got one of the young men, Oscar's friend, off the train and aggressively threw him on the ground by his hair and wrist. He was not resisting.

When Oscar saw what the officer was doing to his friend, he spoke up and asked to talk to someone in charge. The officer on site did not like that and ran over and hit Oscar. Oscar sat back down.

Oscar's fiancée had gone downstairs to the restroom. He was taking such a long time to come down, so she called his cell phone at about 2:09 a.m. He answered and told her, "They are beating us up for no reason." She asked who, and he told her "the police." Oscar hung up the phone, and the situation would get ugly quickly.

His friends' story continued.

Oscar tells his friends to be quiet, "Follow their instructions, and do what they say, and we're going home tonight. Just be quiet."

There were only two officers on-site at the platform at first, and now, four or five officers were on the platform at the BART Station. One of the officers who was on the platform pointed his Taser at Oscar, and Oscar said, "Man, I have a four-year-old daughter." Oscar then snaps a photo of him pointing his Taser at him. It would be the last photo on Oscar's phone.

His fiancée calls him back. He quickly answers and tells her he has to go.

The lead officer instructs the officer who'd pointed the Taser at Oscar to restrain him and his friend. So, they attempt to restrain Oscar but laid him on his friend's feet, and his hands are trapped underneath him. His friend is yelling, "He's on my leg."

The Lead officer, who weighs about 300 pounds, puts his knee on Oscar's neck. Oscar yells, "I can't breathe." The other officer is at Oscar's feet. He's also very large. Both were twice Oscar's size, and he only weighed about 160 pounds.

Oscar tries to breathe, squirming, and lies flat, facedown, as instructed.

While restraining Oscar, an officer—positioned at his feet—stands up abruptly, takes out his pistol, and fires.

The bullet leaves the chamber and enters Oscar's back. Later, we'd find it entered his lungs and blows one of his lungs out.

Oscar lies there. The crowd hears POW! A gunshot. The shot that caused Oscar to yell out, "You shot me! I have a four-year-old daughter."

Oscar lay bleeding on the cold concrete platform at the Fruitvale BART Station in Oakland, California. Red blood oozed out of Oscar onto the pavement. Blood oozed out of his mouth. He was beginning to bleed out.

His friends were horrified, terrified, wondering what and why it happened. What will happen next? Will they also be shot?

The entire platform became silent for a few minutes. The passengers on the BART train looked on, filming the horrifying event. A passenger shouted, "You shot him. I got you, MFer." She filmed the entire incident. The crowd starts screaming, "Oh my God, you shot him. You just shot him." Everyone is in disbelief.

His friends yelled, "You shot him!" One threw a cell phone.

While Oscar lay on the platform, one of his friends kept telling him to "keep your eyes open." Another friend tells him to "keep talking. You'll be all right."

The ambulance finally arrived, and the driver reported Oscar was still coherent as he lay bleeding out on the concrete. Per the ambulance driver and his friends, he was talking and conscious on his way to the hospital.

I could not believe the story I was being told. I just knew that it wasn't an officer hired to protect and serve who had shot Oscar. I thought it must be a dream or nightmare, not my son lying there restrained and still shot in the back. *Who would do such a hateful thing in front of a crowd of people?* I could not fathom it.

I wondered what Oscar felt at that moment. Was he thinking about all that he learned about God? About his daughter and fiancée? His mother and sister? Was he praying? At twenty-two years old, he had just started a new year. At 11:59 p.m. on New Year's Eve, Oscar received a text from his uncle telling him "Happy New Year. Uncle loves you." His uncle never received a text back.

Chapter 7

The Last Turn of Fate

Oscar's friends, who were on the platform with him at the BART Station, were taken to BART's holding jail for questioning. His other friends were already at the hospital. When we arrived, some of Oscar's friend's parents were there to meet me.

I went into the chapel and prayed while doctors were operating on Oscar. When I returned to the visitors room, a social worker told me how serious his injury was, life-threatening. I now believe she was preparing me for the worst, that I would not see Oscar alive again.

I called some family and friends to let them know what happened. I wanted to call my pastor then, even dialing the number, but hung up the phone. It was too late or too early to call. I tried to call another friend several times, and it went straight to voice mail. Another friend answered my call, asking what

I wanted her to do. I didn't want her to come, but I needed her to pray.

My best friend, who was like a sister I had known for over fifteen years, screamed at the news. She did not listen about coming to the hospital. My best friend, her husband, and her daughter arrived so quick, I believe he must have been driving at least 100 miles per hour.

He was one of the men who attended Palma Ceia Baptist Church and a male figure in Oscar's life. He helped me with Oscar when he was younger. A no-nonsense father, he knew how to keep Oscar in line and did not allow him to talk back. He demanded obedience, and Oscar was respectful when he was with them at their home. My god-niece, their daughter, was also close to Oscar. They grew up together and both attended private schools in their elementary years.

My niece, my sister's daughter, came to the hospital, and all I recall was her hitting the wall and screaming.

More family, his friends and mine, his friends' parents, arrived at the hospital. The emotions in the hospital were so high. Everyone was dealing with what happened to Oscar in their own way. His friends were so upset.

His other friends were still being detained at the BART Station holding jail. I wasn't sure why when it was later told to us that they were not under arrest.

I asked everyone to come together, and we held hands and prayed. I said, "God, You are the Creator of Heaven and Earth. All things consist of You, and You made all things. You created Oscar and can heal him if it is Your will. I ask You, God, to touch his body and cause the bleeding to stop and cause him to live and not die. Touch the doctors and give them the wisdom to do their job well. Touch the nurses in the room that are working on Oscar. Lord, touch everyone in this circle and strengthen each of us. We come together, lifting Oscar, asking for healing in Jesus' name. God, I ask You to touch his lungs and cause them to operate as You created them. I ask Father God to move in his life and bring healing in Jesus' name, amen."

I told everyone Oscar needed us to be strong for him. We filled the waiting room. His friends were finally released from being held for over five hours in BART's holding cells. They headed to the hospital.

I asked his friends who were on the platform when he was shot what happened. They told me the story again.

A nurse came into the waiting room and asked me to accompany her. When I first entered the room to see Oscar, I remember two BART police officers sitting outside his door. I told them there was no way they were stopping us from seeing my son. There was quiet. No response. My sister went with me into the room. Oscar was hooked up to several different machines. He had just come out of surgery and was heavily sedated, so he didn't know we were in the room. My sister talked to Oscar, rubbed his head, held his hand, and kissed him. She said, "Nephew, I love you." I, too, started talking to him. I began praying, asking God to heal him.

My sister and I walked out of the room to get his fiancée to see him. Before I could get all the words out, the nurse called me back into the room. She insisted that I hurry. The two BART police officers were still sitting there with a laptop. When I walked back into the room, hospital staff were trying to resuscitate

Oscar. The doctors were working hard to keep him from slipping into eternity. I held my stomach and tried to keep from letting out a scream, but couldn't hold it. I tried to fight back the tears as I watched. They were doing everything to keep him alive. One doctor said, "The more blood we pump into him, the more blood he's losing." It was like a faucet with a leak; the water keeps dripping even when it's off. Their efforts were unsuccessful.

There were the doctors and a police officer in the room while Oscar was being resuscitated.

I watched my son take his last breath. They pronounced Oscar dead before sunrise on January 1, 2009, in the very same hospital where his precious life began.

I had to leave the room and regroup to tell everyone that Oscar went to be with the Lord. It was the hardest thing for me ever to do. I walked back into the visitors room and hugged my daughter, and she knew. She said, "No, Mom." And I said, "Yes." She cried.

There were about forty people waiting to hear Oscar's status. The wailing was indescribable. Everyone held each other, crying, yelling, screaming, and sobbing. I wanted to go back and see Oscar one more time but was told they had to treat it like a murder. So, I was forbidden to enter his room again.

I returned to the waiting room, and everyone was still crying and consoling each other. I could not believe it. One of my employees, whom I had known for over twenty years, arrived. She hugged me, and we cried. I could not believe she had come. I teased her about it because it was her first time in Oakland, California, and she lived ten miles south in Hayward, California. When she heard the news, she said she could not stay away. I was so grateful to see her face.

The family and friends stayed another hour and then began leaving. My best friend stayed with me until I was ready to leave.

Chapter 8

A Story Worthy of Reporting

To our surprise, we walked out the hospital door, and the media from every station was there. Channels 2, 7, 4, 5 and Telemundo. Local newspaper agencies were there as well, looking to get an interview. One of the local station's reporters asked if he could have an interview and stuck his camera in my face. My best friend put her hand out, right over the lens, and grabbed me. We kept walking to the car.

When we arrived at my mother's house, news station vans were parked in the front yard. Reporters were parked all around.

At first, we did not realize that a video had been given to the news outlets. Four videos and countless photos from cell phones had been uploaded onto YouTube. There were over a million views, with hundreds of negative and positive comments. Today, there have been over 4.3M views (as of December, 2023) watching the killing of my son on YouTube. The comments ranged from calling Oscar a thug and a criminal to so many other racial slurs. More positive comments were he was murdered and that he was a father. We found out why the media wanted to interview us. They wanted to know how we felt about the videos.

The media parked in front of my mother's house for several days, trying for an interview. I could not believe how quickly the news of what happened to Oscar spread.

That evening, the phone kept ringing from several attorneys offering their services. An attorney approached my parents' house. He wanted to know if I wanted to retain his services. I'm not even sure how he found out. I don't even recall whether a family member called him or if I called him. I ended up hiring him as my attorney. It's interesting now that I look back. I had an attorney before I even had the funeral.

I was glad my best friend was there to answer some of the questions and calls I received. She began writing down messages and returning phone calls for me.

I can share now that when situations like what happened to Oscar occur, you are not thinking. Things are hard to process. People start to come around you, and you're unclear about what you should or should not do. Having someone around you who is rational and can think clearly is important because It may be hard to make rational decisions. Often, when something of this magnitude happens, the family talks to reporters and attorneys without thinking the situation through clearly. I am not saying it is wrong; what I am saying is because of the person's state of mind, they may not have an opportunity to process things logically. This is when families must band together with friends to help determine the course of action that must be taken. It's good to appoint a spokesperson for the family with only one point of contact.

I sat numb on the first day when we were ready to plan the funeral, and my best friend stayed over for hours. She had been with me all early morning and day. She finally went home, only to change clothes. I am sure she was tired, but that did not stop her from coming back.

She returned every day for about two weeks. She helped me by thinking of things that needed to be done. Knowing my frame of mind, she answered my phone and helped with what I needed. From morning to evening, she was there with me. Waiting on me. The Lord really used her to be a blessing to me and my family. I could not thank her enough. I think back now, not knowing how I would have done it without her.

Chapter 9
It's So Hard to Say Goodbye

After the second day, we began to plan the funeral. We knew we would hold the service at Palma Ceia Baptist Church, where we attended as a family. The men in the church had played a significant role in Oscar's upbringing. They helped raise Oscar; they took him fishing and on field trips. Oscar professed the Lord Jesus as his Savior at Palma Ceia, and the pastor baptized him. Very active in the church, he sang in the choir, ushered on the usher board, was a royal ambassador, and played for the church's basketball team.

When Oscar turned eighteen, he was an adult and didn't attend worship service regularly. I am sure many parents can identify with this. You raise your child with religious values in the church. You gave them no options; they had to attend church service every Sunday. Then they turn of age or move out and decide they aren't going to attend anymore. This can be frustrating to a parent. You want your child to have a relationship with the Lord. You have tried hard to train them up according to Proverbs 22:6 (KJV). Train up a child in the way he should go: and when he is old, he will not depart from it.

Oscar didn't have a choice. When he was younger, I would wake him and his sister at 6:45 a.m. and prepare for church. He was required to attend Sunday School and church service.

I asked the interim pastor in charge if we could have the funeral at Palma Ceia, and he agreed without hesitation.

I attended two churches at the time, Palma Ceia and Abundant Life New Generation Ministries. The pastor's wife at Abundant Life New Generation Ministries called to inform me the church family would bring food to my mom's house. At 3:00 p.m. that day, the members delivered all types of food and juices. But I was grateful.

Different auxiliaries from Palma Ceia called, wanting to know what they could do. The minister of music asked what was needed. Oscar had sung in the Sunshine Choir and the Young Adults Choir. The choir would be prepared to sing. Usher board members would usher during service. I could not believe the outpouring of love and support I was receiving from so many people and different churches.

It was now time to prepare the order of service.

I had several choices of who was to deliver the eulogy. I knew I wanted a man to give the message of comfort to Oscar's friends. Although some capable women pastors would have done an outstanding job, I just felt that a man would identify better with the young men. I had heard the selected pastor preach and was satisfied he could minister to them. Several other pastors were invited to bring words of expression.

I asked Pastor Glo and Co-pastor Word, who knew Oscar, to speak. They'd watched Oscar grow up in the house of the Lord. We'd also attended the same church for many years, but they were no longer members of Palma Ceia. But I recalled the words they'd prophesied concerning Oscar. They called him a *little preacher*. I didn't see what God was showing them at the time. Both pastors shared a story about Oscar and his family. They'd visited Christ

Center Church, where they pastored. They wanted him to attend and join, but Oscar offered the excuse there were no young adults. Pastor Glo told him to go out and bring some young adults back by inviting them to come.

I attempted writing the obituary. It was tough. I'm writing out the obituary for my son when my son should be writing the obituary for me. I couldn't think of my son's birthdate and entered the wrong date. In between the crying inside, I couldn't think. My best friend caught the mistake and took the note paper. "Let me do this." So, she finished writing it and had her daughter's friend and another mutual friend complete the edits and add pictures.

McNary, Williams & Jackson Funerals would prepare the body and handle the burial. One of the owners attended Palma Ceia. I was supposed to go to the mortuary to view his body, but could not muster up enough strength. I still wondered and wanted to turn the clock back.

My best friend knew what needed to be done for the funeral, so she made a list, and we started completing the rest of her tasks. I needed to select clothes for Oscar, and she had my brother step in to shop and pick out the clothing. My brother's friend groomed him, shaved and cut his hair. I could not imagine performing those tasks or watching someone else dress him. Next, we had to set things for the funeral in place. It seemed like the questions would never stop. We had to decide the type of casket or if we wanted to cremate. What area of the cemetery did we want his body buried? What words are engraved on the headstone? Limousines? A procession, escorts? Question after question, I was so glad when we'd selected the casket and headstone. We'd finished and I was in a daze already.

All I remember is that the prices kept getting higher and higher. We were at over fifteen thousand dollars by the time everything was done. So many options to choose from. Thus, the importance of having someone with you thinking more clearly than the immediate family member. I was also glad we had an insurance policy. I now encourage families I encounter to ensure they have a policy for their loved ones. My best friend paid for the headstone; she was there with me and my mother and knew I wasn't thinking clearly. Or my shell of a body was there, but my mind had checked out. I sat there and wept; my heart was still aching and longing for Oscar. Tears still flowed no matter what my son and I went through in life. *He was still my child.*

We returned to the house, and Abundant Life New Generation Ministries Church family delivered more food. Friends and family were coming and going throughout the day and even until evening. My best friend started a list of who visited or called and what they brought: flowers, plants, food, or cards. Later, sending thank you cards wouldn't be complicated.

Another friend took care of getting Oscar's friends together for pallbearers. We had more than enough pallbearers in black tuxedos.

It did not matter what I wore, but I remember deciding on a black and gray dress.

So many mixed thoughts flooded my mind. Who would I get to turn out my light for me? Who would pick up food from the grocery store? Oscar had always turned out my bedroom light when he was home.

The funeral

We held the funeral on January 7, 2009, at Palma Ceia Baptist Church in Hayward, California. The bereavement pastor officiated the service, and one of the interim pastors delivered the eulogy. I decided not to have a quiet hour. To me, it's like having a funeral, and I didn't want to endure the pain twice. The funeral service was the last time anyone would see Oscar's face. The last time to say *see you later, see you on the other side.*

We arrived at the church, and the media had beaten us there. They were interviewing people attending the funeral. As I exited the car, I told myself this was not real. It cannot be honest; I was there in body, but it seemed like I was having an out-of-body experience.

I had not seen Oscar alive since December 31, 2008, my birthday. I hadn't gone to the funeral home and would view my son's body for the first and last time at the funeral. He lay stiff as a board, lifeless. I touched him, and he did not even look like himself. I looked at him from head to toe. No smile, no movement. I prayed to God, asking him to cause him to rise from the dead.

His swollen face and hands looked different. His skin had turned dark brown. I told Chantay it didn't look like Oscar. I kept telling myself *this was not real. This was not Oscar. What happened to my son?* Chantay viewed Oscar's body and sobbed uncontrollably. My brother and her father consoled her. She cried and screamed.

So many things went on during the funeral. With over a thousand people there, there was standing room only. People came from all over. Just as many outside as inside. The pastor eulogized Oscar, and a sister from Palma Ceia sang "What About the Children." Several people spoke, and my pastor's daughter praise-danced. Before the pastor finished the message, some of Oscar's friends walked out of the church. For them, the funeral was over.

Oscar's body could be viewed one last time before the burial. It's my turn. I didn't want to see him; I wanted this dream to end. I saw his body for the last time. I kissed him. Oscar's spirit was already gone to be with the Lord. What I was looking at was only his shell. I thought about 2 Corinthians 5:1 (KJV). For we know that if our earthly house of this tabernacle were dissolved, we have a building of God, a house not made with hands, eternal in the heavens.

I also thought about 2 Corinthians 5:8 (KJV): We are confident, I say, and willing rather to be absent from the body, and to be present with the Lord. Oscar was present with the Lord. His physical house was still here. I said, *Why did he have to die?*

We exited the church and drove towards the cemetery followed by a van full of flowers. We received so many flowers from all over. BART Board members, KFC, my job UPS, and several of my friends sent flowers and plants. After the funeral, I gave away flowers and plants; there were too many to take home. The remaining had my mother's living room looking like a nursery.

At the cemetery, cameras and news crews were all around. The media followed everywhere we went.

The pastor said, "Death is a part of life, and we have come to the end of the road with Oscar. We can go no further with him. Earth to earth, ashes to ashes, dust to dust." As directed, Oscar's friends laid the pallbearers' gloves on his casket. I laid a flower petal atop the casket, then Chantay, Sophina, and Titiana.

We all wept. One of Oscar's friends threw bills on top of the casket. I told him sometime later that Oscar didn't need the money. He could have given the money to me. His friends wailed and sobbed. After the pastor's closing prayer, workers lowered Oscar into the ground. Family helped me to the car, sobbing and saying to myself, *I will never get to see my baby boy again.*

We returned to Palma Ceia for the repast sponsored by KFC, Palma Ceia, Abundant Life New Generation Ministries and Farmer Joe's where Oscar worked. Managers and employees from both jobs attended.

After a few hours, and everyone had left, I faced going home to deal with a new life after my loss. Now, I had to pick up the shattered pieces.

Chapter 10

Picking Up The Pieces

I felt broken into pieces, not knowing how to process what had happened. Still wondering about Oscar's thoughts at the moment he was shot. Continually hearing, "You shot me. I have a four-year-old daughter."

There were questions I wish I had answers to. So many thoughts I could not get out of my mind.

What was the BART officer thinking when he shot Oscar in the back? Perhaps the stress of working on a night he should've taken off to be with his fiancée. She was laboring to give birth to his child while he was taking the life of another woman's child. He pulled a gun instead of the Taser he said he meant to draw. That we'll never know.

Oscar would never implement his New Year's resolution to make it to barber school. Or see the sun rise on the first day of a brand new year. He'd never fulfill his twenty-one goals. He'd never have another chance to kiss his mama or daughter. Or marry his fiancée. Watch Tatiana grow up and graduate. Never play basketball against his nephew Leroy. Or watch him graduate from high school.

Instead, Oscar's life was punctured by a bullet from a gun allegedly pulled as a Taser. If not for hundreds of BART riders who watched and documented the fatal shot, you likely wouldn't know about Oscar or myself. I'm the mother whose heart may now resemble a kintsugi bowl—a bowl made from a form of Japanese art that mends fragments of broken pieces into something whole. Like biblical Rizpah, I'll fight for those pieces and measures of justice, not stopping until there is justice for all.

You may not know me personally, but I stand on the front line for all children. I faced a period of overwhelming grief, replaying Oscar's death, wishing I had not told him to take BART.

Have you ever felt so guilty of doing something that the discomfort was unbearable? The spirit of guilt brings you to a place where you feel the incident occurred because of you.

That feeling leads to depression. Severe despondency and dejection, constant sadness, and loss of interest, which stops you from performing your normal activities. I felt so broken inside. There were days I could not think, could not eat, and did not want to get out of bed. I was sinking further into depression.

There are many types of depression, the mood caused by the persistent feeling of sadness, hopelessness, and self-pity. Depression can also destroy any belief you have in God. It affects your ability to think, feel, and function. It made me not want to go to church where my roots were. I would stay home on Sundays and Bible Study nights and not attend worship services. I went deeper into a hole, isolating myself. Not answering the phone, including church folks whose solution was to praise God.

It made me feel like I had not been praying to God about my son, and He had heard nothing I prayed. Have you ever felt like you were praying about something, and the prayer was not answered, for whatever reason? Like God was not hearing or listening? You wanted to stop praying.

Keep praying. I recall a mother's testimony about God's goodness in reviving her son who'd been shot.

After he'd code-blued, God heard her prayer. I felt some way the devil was talking in my ear, saying, "See, you weren't praying. God doesn't hear you when you pray." The devil was trying to take me to a place where there would be no coming back. This happens to some people who find themselves praying about a situation, and for whatever reason, the prayer request has not been answered. They believe it is their fault that their prayer has not come to pass. I remembered what John 10:10 (KJV) reads. The thief cometh not, but for to steal, and to kill, and to destroy: I am come that they might have life, and that they might have it more abundantly.

I remember praying while lying on the bed, fighting depression. This was more than a physical battle. It was a spiritual battle. The scripture in Psalm 34:1 (KJV) came to me. I will bless the Lord at all times: and his praise shall continually be in my mouth.

I had no idea how I could praise God with Oscar gone. So, I thanked Him for Oscar and for letting me be his mother for the twenty-two years he lived. The good, the bad, the beautiful, and the ugly. I encourage you to thank God right now. Don't focus on the situation. Focus on the One larger than the situation.

God already knew and soon reminded me of what He told me years ago. Oscar would go through some things, and we would be in ministry together. I wondered how we could be in ministry together when he was dead. But I could hear God speaking to me. *Was He speaking audibly?*

No, I could sense in spirit Him reminding me that the people I was seeing and those who would read these pages were not because of me. But because of the loss of my son. A reminder that we are in ministry together.

Our ministry is to travel this country, offering hope to families and communities who have faced losses due to police and community violence. Losing a loved one can never be easy, but turning your pain and tragedy into triumph to purpose will benefit the entire community. I found that no matter how you pick up the pieces, you still find yourself dealing with the reality of your loved one being gone. And you deal with the five-letter word that has five cycles, which we call *grief*.

Chapter 11

Falling Into A Hole

Grief is a natural response to death or loss. The grieving process is an opportunity to mourn the loss and then heal. When you think about grief, the trauma can be so overwhelming that you feel guilty and blame yourself for the loss. The loss does not have to be the loss of a human. It could be a relationship or maybe a job.

Guilt and blame are some of the responses from grief that I felt. You might feel some other type of emotion. I felt guilty and blamed myself for what happened to my son. He would still be with us today if I had not told him to take BART. I blamed, I bargained with God, asking Him why my son and not me. I felt my emotions were so up, down, and all around. Friends have said, it's like being on a roller coaster that you can't get off of.

The stages are fundamental. I went through each and still go through them. The denial, the anger, the bargaining, the depression, and the acceptance. These are said to be the five stages of grief. You go through each without a set order or time limit. Or you may go through the stages simultaneously.

Every person deals with grief differently, so I can only share how I went through this new way of life that I was experiencing. No longer was I able to ask Oscar to turn off my light. I now had to do it myself. Grief makes you pick up the pieces that the one who is no longer here once picked up.

The stages of grief range from denial to acceptance.

Denial of initial shock and disbelief is often a coping mechanism for overwhelming emotions.

Anger: Frustration and resentment directed towards oneself, others, or the situation.

Bargaining: Attempts to negotiate or make deals to reverse or lessen the impact of loss.

Depression: Intense feelings of sadness and despair as the reality of the loss sets in.

Acceptance: Coming to terms with the loss and finding a way to move forward with life.

It's important to note the stages are not necessarily experienced linearly. Individuals may go through them differently or revisit certain stages. Grief can cause you to feel up and down with mixed emotions.

Dealing with grief, I found I could not control the tears that continued to flow. The pain was insufferable. I could not eat. I could not sleep. When would this nightmare be over? When would this dream end? I cried out to God, asking Him to take the pain away. To remove the hurt. Only He knew the pain I was enduring. I alternated through the five stages of grief—mad one day, bargaining the next day, depression, acceptance, and denial. My emotions were everywhere, like I was on a rollercoaster and couldn't get off.

Most people who experience a death go through these stages. Not everyone experiences them in the same order. I experienced the emotion of guilt for years, which is not one of the stages but an emotion. I was drowning in guilt. I knew it wasn't my fault, but if only I could reverse the clock. If only I could change the time, I would return to my December 31,

2008 birthday. I found myself praying, asking God to remove this guilt.

The pain of guilt only lessened when I forgave myself. Guilt is an emotional state that arises from a belief that one has violated a moral standard or has done something wrong. It often involves a sense of remorse. Self-reproach, or regret for actions or behaviors that go against personal values or societal norms.

I had to forgive myself for telling Oscar to take the BART, which was the right thing to do. Forgiveness is a conscious decision to release feelings of resentment or vengeance toward a person or oneself who has caused harm. It doesn't necessarily condone the actions, but frees the forgiver from the burden of carrying negative emotions. Guilt and blame can be so overwhelming that one chooses not to forgive themselves. Not doing so can cause sickness to attach itself to your body. It can lead to shame, guilt, low self-esteem, hurt, anxiety, and, in the end, death can occur. Not forgiving yourself can cause you to go into a deep well of depression.

If you feel guilty today, I encourage you to forgive yourself and let it go. It is not your fault. I found the only way to really move forward is to forgive yourself and not allow the blame to hold and weigh you down. Once you do so, you can move with God's purpose. Ephesians 4:32 (KJV). And be ye kind one to another, tenderhearted forgiving one another, even as God for Christ's sake hath forgiven you.

It was the very words that I needed to hear from my mother that helped me realize it was not my fault. She reminded me that the God of this universe knew what would happen to Oscar before January 1, 2009. If I believed in what I preached, I needed to stand on that. I was reminded of all God had shown me years ago concerning Oscar and me.

Chapter 12

Walking In Purpose

One Sunday, I'd gone to worship at Abundant Life New Generation Ministries. The female pastor approached to pray for me. She said God told her to cancel out some things coming up against me, and to deliver His assignment for me. She denounced spirits that were trying to distract me because I had so many things on my mind. The Lord instructed her to assassinate, pull down, annihilate those bad spirits. And to pray over my mind strength, fortitude, and vision to be crystal clear with discernment.

My assignment was justice; The pastor could see my mouth being used as a weapon to speak against injustice. She prayed for my feet because of the places I was going to be sent.

While doing this in her spirit, she heard the Holy Spirit say, "I call her Rizpah." She kept praying and heard it two more times. The Spirit directed her to follow as instructed. She wasn't sure what the name was, but obeyed God and called forth "Rizpah."

She was unsure if It might be a city, someone or something. So, she anointed my hands, feet, mouth, ears, eyes, and heart. I cried and sobbed.

She asked her co-pastor, her husband, if he knew the name Rizpah. He did not. So, she searched Google, finding the passage in the Bible. All she could say was "Oh my God!" She called on another pastor, one of our mutual friends in the Lord. They both read the passage several times. It was so divine because God was having her pray this over me six months after Oscar had been gone. Then reading about Rizpah, who fanned and watched over her sons' dead bodies for six months.

Maybe you have not heard of the story of Rizpah, so I want to share a portion of it with you. The rest you'll want to read at the end of this book.

Two Samuel 21.

We meet **Rizpah**, a mother grieving over the untimely deaths of her two sons. Through her silence, they confront us with the uncomfortable realities accompanying inequitable power distribution. Yet,

Rizpah's silence, as a powerful testimony of a mother's pain, love, and courage, reassures us to be steadfast in our faith since God can turn our most tragic moments into our greatest triumphs.

2 Samuel 21:8-11-12 (CEV)

But Saul and Rizpah, the daughter of Aiah, had two sons named Armoni and Mephibosheth. Saul's daughter Merab had five sons whose father was Adriel, the son of Barzillai from Meholah. David took Rizpah's two sons and Merab's five sons and turned them over to the Gibeonites, who hanged all seven of them on the mountain near the place where the Lord was worshiped. This happened right at the beginning of the barley harvest. Rizpah spread out some sackcloth on a nearby rock. She wouldn't let the birds land on the bodies during the day, and she kept the wild animals away at night. She stayed there from the beginning of the harvest until it started to rain.

Now, Rizpah and I had a goal in mind; we both wanted to see justice for our sons. Like Rizpah, I did not want the community to think or say that Oscar got what he deserved. I felt and believed that Oscar did not do anything wrong on that dreadful morning to deserve his life to be snatched from him. I felt that he did not deserve to be tased. I only wanted justice; I wanted the officer to pay for his crime, even if that meant prison. If it had been your child, I am sure you probably would have felt the same. Rizpah's sons were killed for nothing they had done wrong. I felt the same way about Oscar.

Rizpah wanted justice for her sons. She watched their bodies hang on a tree. She saw their bodies change colors and even decay. I am sure their bodies were probably starting to stink. But Rizpah remained right there, holding a vigil daily for her sons. Rizpah was determined not to stop until she received the justice her sons deserved. Rizpah had to protect her sons in death from violence. She had to fight off the scavenger's night and day. fighting to ensure no animals landed on their bodies or harmed them. Though Rizpah felt trauma, grief, and sadness, she did not let that stop her from pursuing justice.

I learned from Rizpah's story not to allow anyone or anything to get in the way of me getting justice for Oscar. The fight for justice requires perseverance, consistency, resilience, and remaining committed to ensuring justice is rendered.

Rizpah received the justice she wanted. A proper burial for her sons. She loved them so much that—through her grief—she fought until they were laid to rest.

I could not believe it, but after I read Rizpah's story for myself, I began to feel that it was genuinely divine that Oscar did not die in vain. But, like Jesus, there was a purpose in his death. Jesus' purpose in death was so that all mankind would come to the knowledge of knowing and accepting him as their personal Savior. Oscar's death was to bring awareness to others that Blacks are still treated differently when stopped by law enforcement.

My question to you is, what if that were your child? If you or I had killed someone, we would have been in jail as soon as the police found out we committed a crime. The bail would be set so high that we would not have money to bail out.

Some people may disagree, but the truth is that Blacks are still being killed at a higher rate than any other nationality. When we look at the statistics, there is an undeniable disparity with Blacks being killed, incarcerated, and stopped at higher rates.

WANDA JOHNSON

Chapter 13
Community Rally Cry For Justice

After the video of Oscar's death was aired by the news media, a Minister from the Nation of Islam called another Minister based in Oakland, California and asked, "What are you going to do about it?" By this time, the video was uploaded on YouTube and being broadcast on KVTU Channel 2. Religious leaders gathered to discuss what occurred and the next course of action. The meeting was held on January 3, 2009, days before the funeral. A group of men and women came together at Olivet Missionary Institutional Baptist Church to discuss the issues leading to the destruction of youth in Oakland, California.

Three days later, community leaders, pastors, public officials, and city council members came together again to strategize on their next course of action. Everyone had seen the video and knew in their hearts what happened to Oscar was unjust and flat-out murder. Community leaders and grass-roots community galvanized. They rallied—over 150 people—and arrived at the Alameda County Courthouse for a press conference scheduled at 9:00 a.m. The leaders included several pastors, Oakland City Council members, NAACP members, California Assembly members, Oakland Mayor, and a California Congresswoman.

District Attorney Tom Orloff was reluctant to press charges. But the community leaders insisted charges be filed against the officer. A Council member appealed that the point needed to be made the district attorney must respect the constituency and prosecute all law enforcement involved in the murder of Oscar Grant.

At the press conference, one of the clergy members cried out, "I am Oscar Grant." The community heard his words, and it became a famous rallying cry from a diverse group of people for all who have been killed at the hands of police. *I am Oscar Grant* began being chanted fourteen years ago in Oakland, California and is still heard today.

The community protested from the first day Oscar was killed until there was a charge. Then the community held Town Hall meetings to determine if they should continue the protest. They protested day after day. Some of the protests were peaceful, while some ended in looting stores, burning cars, and setting things on fire.

I was so surprised to receive a phone call from Mayor Dellums. He wanted me to tell the protestors "...not to protest the loss of my son, not to loot."

I responded, "The people are going to do what they want. No matter how much I tell them not to riot or loot, they will not listen to me."

The protesters walked on Interstate 880 and shut the freeway down. They went to the BART Station and disrupted the services. The protesters were not returning to business as usual; they demanded that the officer be charged. Something had to be done.

There was a meeting with the district attorney. It's believed he underestimated the group's power. The group had no name, and no leader had been identified. They all recognized the need to ensure Oscar Grant and his family received the justice they deserved.

Another press conference was held at the Alameda County Courthouse. Expressing outrage, the growing group demanded the district attorney meet with them. So much pressure was exerted that he said he'd meet with only a select few people from the group. The group banded together, and "all or none" was their reply. While he continued to refuse, more press conferences were held.

The district attorney finally agreed to a meeting. The impressive group of leaders and supporters included: community, religious and city, state and national political leadership, ministers and members of the Nation of Islam, and NAACP state representatives. The group demanded that the district attorney file charges.

Still insisting he wouldn't file charges, however, after the pressure mounted, he finally reconsidered. During the meeting, he informed community leaders the officers were given time to work out their defense. By now, it was clear the defense would include a smear campaign against Oscar to make him look like he deserved to be killed.

It is sad because often when African American young men are killed, a smear campaign begins. Too often it works. When Trayvon Martin was killed, the campaign centered on his being suspended from school and a few other things. When Eric Garner was killed, the focus was him selling *loosies* cigarettes. And when George Floyd was killed, a campaign was set up against him as well. Often, once they're introduced, it causes citizens to make decisions on whether they feel the individual deserved what happened to them. Unfortunately, potential jurors hearing the negatives about the individuals base their decisions on the smear.

District Attorney Orloff charged Officer Johannes Mehserle with second-degree murder. I don't believe he wanted to, because soon after, he retired.

The community continued working to get justice for Oscar. A busload of community activists went to Sacramento and shared what happened to Oscar. They were determined not to allow what happened to him to be forgotten. They wanted a charge *and* a conviction.

Mehserle was in Las Vegas and had to return to California. He claimed his reasoning for fleeing California was he feared for his life. He was extradited and then booked into Santa Rita County Jail. A bail was set at three million dollars. The Chief of Police of BART set up a GoFundMe page, leading efforts to raise funds for Mehserle to be released from jail. He received enough donations from the police union, friends and family efforts to have him released. The chief received tremendous backlash for starting the page, and soon retired.

One of the television stations interviewed the officer while he was held in jail. I could not believe how even the media tried to help him appeal to potential jurors.

I knew the fight to get the officer convicted would be an uphill battle. This was the first time in California history that an on-duty officer had faced charges for an on-duty shooting. Only by prayer would he be convicted.

Minister Louis Farrakhan spoke with the ministers of the Nation of Islam and arranged a trip to Oakland. A historic visit, he arrived on February 17 for the meeting at Olivet Missionary Baptist Church. The house was packed: no seating room. People stood all over with great anticipation of what Minister Farrakhan would speak. Oscar's killing stirred something that had been building up in Oakland for a long time. In his hour-long speech, Farrakhan said to Oscar's "beautiful mother and the father she fathered a child with, don't fret. Don't grieve. Don't think they can get away from that universal law that's not dependent on crooked law and prosecutors and police chiefs who don't do their jobs." The audience applauded,.giving him standing ovations several times. He challenged the crowd to pursue justice for Oscar.

I did not attend the service but heard all about it and listened to it on YouTube. I was genuinely amazed and hated I hadn't attended. I remember so clearly him saying, "This mother will be the winner."

The Minister would declare several times I would be the *winner*. At that moment, I felt I had won. As mentioned, it was the first time in California history that an officer was charged with an on-duty shooting.

Now, my family had to prepare for the court proceedings. The community was willing to assist wherever was necessary to ensure we were there.

Chapter 14

Change of Venue

The court proceedings began in Oakland, California. We went to court Monday through Friday. The defendant's attorney, motioned to move the trial to Los Angeles. He said his client could not receive an impartial jury.

I disagreed. I believed the Oakland Bay area people would make the right decision and render a guilty or innocent verdict. The citizens in Alameda County had a right to consider a verdict. But, it did not matter what I thought should happen, the judge would have the final say.

The defense request for a change of venue was submitted. We prayed and waited for the judge's decision. The motion was accepted to move the trial. The options were San Diego or Southern California. I did not want the trial to move to San Diego, which was much further than Los Angeles. Also, San Diego was a more military city, and I felt a pro-police county. The judge moved the trial to Southern California, the Los Angeles County Courthouse.

Now, we would have to plan our travel to Los Angeles. Driving or flying, then driving from the airport. Although Los Angeles was preferred, expense-wise it was horrible. Another expense. A four hundred mile, five to six-hour trip. Then a place to stay for the week. I even had to pay attorney fees for my civil suit attorney to fly to Los Angeles to listen to the questioning. That might help if we got to trial for the civil suit. So, the expenses were piling up. We had paid the funeral expense, and now the costs to be present at my son's court proceedings.

On the first day of court, I was pleased at the scene when we arrived at the Los Angeles courthouse. There were protestors with signs demanding justice for Oscar. Signs that read I am Oscar Grant. Other signs read Guilty, Charge Killer Cops, Justice for Oscar Grant, and Charge all Racist Killer Cops. Protestors wore tee shirts with pictures of Oscar, and some carried signs with photos of Oscar. Whole Damn System is Guilty signs were posted everywhere.

Los Angeles protestors had shown up to support us. Activists from the Bay Area also drove down to Los Angeles. Alameda County, Bay Area and Los Angeles had joined forces. The activists rallied daily and waited for my family and friends to exit the court. The judge was not impressed with the activism.

There was a lot of media presence as well. On the first day of court, a motion was made to allow the media to record the proceedings, and Judge Robert J. Perry rejected the request. He made it clear there would be no outbursts in his courtroom. He believed Johannes Mehserle, the former police officer, did not intend to use his gun, but mistook it for his Taser. The judge clearly expressed his opinions concerning the case plenty of times. We wanted the court system to treat us fairly, but I believe the judge had already decided the outcome. From that point on, we knew we would not receive a fair trial.

After the first day in court, the only way we'd get any conviction was if God put it on the jurors' hearts to judge fairly. I thought about a scripture in the book of Micah, Chapter 6:8 (KJV) that reads, He hath shewed thee, O man what is good; and what does the

Lord require of thee, but to do justly, and to love mercy, and to walk humbly with your God?

Each day, we prayed before court, and after the press conferences, the day ended with prayer. More than just a physical battle, I believed from the beginning it would be a spiritual battle.

The courtroom would only seat a few people. Each day at 7 a.m., there was a lottery pick. Everyone was given a raffle ticket to drop in a bucket. If your ticket number was called, you were allowed in the courtroom. Sometimes, my family members were not picked. It wasn't very pleasant to me that they'd driven five to six hours only to be denied access to the proceedings. Being in a place where we weren't welcome was hard.

We were instructed inside the courtroom we could not wear tee shirts or any item that had pictures of Oscar. No signs were allowed.

The Judge seemed more troubled about the protestors than what had happened to Oscar. He kept saying he wanted them to be gone. He threatened to make the proceedings last a year or five years if the protestors remained outside protesting.

The judge gave his rules to the attorneys and set a date to begin selecting the jury.

It was time to start looking at the jury pool. *Would we get a fair trial?* I believe the questions were fashioned so most Black potential jurors would be disqualified. Questions like: Do you think police sometimes lie? Have you ever been a victim of racial profiling? Do you know anyone whom the police have ever abused? Do you think the police always tell the truth? Have you ever been stopped by the police?

Most of the potential Black jurors had an encounter with the police or knew someone who had. Their answers almost immediately disqualified them. They were thanked and dismissed. *Was this just a setup? Was anyone going to fight for justice for my son? How could they ask the potential black jurors these questions?* For many Blacks, if they answered the questions truthfully, they would be removed from being a juror. I watched all the Black jurors be dismissed. Someone said that Blacks do not know how to answer the questions when being considered as a juror, and because of this, they are often passed. I understood why I was being told that. All the jurors were selected. Not one Black.

As distasteful as it might be, community members must learn the importance of involving ourselves in the court system functions, such as being a part of the jury pools. We need Black jurors if we want more equitable outcomes.

Chapter 15

Demanding Justice

The trial began on June 10, 2010. Prosecutor David Stein and the defense attorney Micheal Rains submitted motion after motion.

Rains wanted all of Oscar's past offenses entered. He'd paint a picture to the jury to believe Oscar deserved to be killed. The judge allowed them to be used during the trial. When prosecutor Stein requested the officer's record of prior complaints be used, the judge would not allow it.

It seemed like the trial was going on for weeks. We would go home on the weekends, leaving right after the trial on Friday. We would be back in court on Monday morning, and the arguments would begin again. My brother Daryl would drive me sometimes, and my sister-in-law other times. When I rode with her, we would sing all the way to and from Los Angeles. Once, when we were on the way home, my brother was pulled over by the police for speeding. I felt terrible for him being issued a ticket.

In opening statements, the prosecution painted a picture of the officers at the scene being out of control. While the defense attorney portrayed the people on the train platform where Oscar was shot as out of control. He said the crowd was getting louder and louder, and the police officers were scared because they were outnumbered. He said the officers did not know if they would get out of there alive.

The prosecution had Oscar's friend take the stand. At fifteen years old, he had witnessed Oscar being shot. He captured the shooting on his cell phone. Barely in high school, he was young and nervous. He was questioned, and as he recalled what happened to Oscar, he broke down. He was in shock. He had not thought something like that would happen to his friend, his play big brother. The judge halted his testimony and called for a break. He did not want the witnesses crying on the stand to influence the jurors' empathy and render a guilty verdict.

The defense attorney kept bringing expert witnesses on the stand who would argue about taser gun confusion. I kept thinking, *how could it be taser gun confusion when Oscar's last picture on his cell phone was of the officer who killed him pointing his Taser at him?* The experts talked about the brain, the hands, and how the officer pulled the wrong weapon. To me, it seemed like excuse after excuse was being made.

One of the expert witnesses for the officer admitted he was being paid for testifying. Another defense witness testified that what you see in the videos is not really what is happening. He said the cellphone video was playing faster than the incident. He'd put a video together slowing down the frame of the shooting, attempting to show Oscar trying to hit the officer.

What? I sat there in disbelief. I kept saying to myself, *why can't they see what I see?*

I wasn't sure why we needed to go through all of this when we all saw the officer shoot my son. It took him less than ten minutes to shoot Oscar.

The killer of my son took the stand. His attorney described him as lovable, a big teddy bear who'd had poor training. He was voted the most huggable in high school, and he could not be a murderer. His training was so lacking that he could not distinguish between a gun and a taser.

On the stand, Mehserle never apologized. When he was in jail, he wrote a letter to the public saying he was sorry. He was now face-to-face with me. You would think he would have apologized. He never did.

He testified Oscar resisted arrest. And his resisting caused him to pull his weapon. The defense attorney went on to say Oscar being shot was not malicious, but rather a case of not being trained properly. The attorney criticized the short training.

I did not believe anything they said because, at first, the officer was saying he thought my son had a gun. That could not be further from the truth because when the dispatcher called in the incident, she informed the police desk operator there were no guns involved. There were so many lies going back and forth that I could not believe it. Prosecution witnesses had disputed his statement and testified Oscar was not resisting. Matter of fact, he was trying to calm his friends down and told them to follow the instructions of the officers so they could all go home.

Finally, the last lie. Rains called expert witnesses to confirm the tense situation caused the officer not to recall which side his taser was on.

I thought to myself, *these are the people who are hired to protect and serve. The people who are there to defend us.* I sat in the courtroom listening to lie after lie. Some of the things my family and I heard were disheartening and unbelievable. So many negatives that would demonize Oscar. I believe that the defense attorney sought to create a demon image the jury would believe did not deserve to live.

I heard testimony daily, just sitting there holding back the tears. I wanted to scream. One protestor in the room screamed and was cited and jailed for three days. The stress was wearing on me when I came out of the courtroom. I found myself feeling numb all over, and my body felt weak. I was so upset and began shaking. A Councilwoman realized something was happening with me. Someone called 911, and the ambulance took me to the hospital. At first, they thought I was suffering a stroke; my blood pressure was high. A series of tests diagnosed Bell's palsy. My face twisted, and I felt so tired. I stayed a couple of hours at the hospital and was released. The doctor informed me that stress from these types of situations could cause paralysis from Bell's palsy attacks.

Information from the court was leaked to the media and then reported to the public. This, I believe, was another part of the campaign to ensure the officer was not charged, or later convicted. As a family, we began to talk about how the court system uses media and how necessary it is for Black people to have their own media outlets to tell their stories. Before accepting what is being said, we must investigate the situation for ourselves. As a people of color, we have been conditioned to believe what the media reports is true, and very little checking has been done to determine its accuracy. Often the media works with the police force, and when the media reports their side to the audience, it is reported without investigative work being done. This can be misleading to the listeners and cause them to accept the facts reported when, in fact, there are times when what is reported is inaccurate.

FROM TRAGEDY TO TRIUMPH

Chapter 16

A Fourteen Year Sentence

The trial lasted three weeks, and the jury began deliberations on July 1, 2010.

The Oakland and Los Angeles communities were in great anticipation of the findings from the jury. People who had seen the video across the country—even internationally—were waiting for the outcome. The police in Oakland beefed up security and their presence because of what they thought might happen. Mayor Dellums was overly concerned. Police were all around: on roofs as sharpshooters, in tanks. Law enforcement was visible everywhere.

The jurors deliberated for eleven hours and rendered their decision on July 8. The jury of his peers found Johannes Mehserle guilty of involuntary manslaughter and a weapon enhancement charge.

On July 8, 2010, I will never forget. The day a knife went straight through my body after hearing the verdict. My family felt horrible that the officer was not charged with more than involuntary manslaughter. I honestly believe he should have been charged with second degree murder.

The conviction was really surprising because if we study the history of policing, we learn that there were times when the Ku Klux Klan and policing collaborated, and through this collaboration, police learned behaviors that did not line up with the motto protect and serve. Our system has been flawed for so many years.

The sentencing

Judge Perry set November 5 that now-convicted Johannes Mehserle would be sentenced for killing Oscar Grant III. The community and my family thought for sure he would receive at least ten years just because the gun charge was ten years by itself. We were hoping that he received the maximum sentences for both which would have been around fourteen years.

Before sentencing, my family was able to give impact statements, and I will never forget my brother's words. "Judge, I hope you do not throw this case…" he began, and upon finishing, he went to his seat.

I provided my impact statement to the courtroom, introducing the judge and jurors to the real human being Oscar—so different from the demon they'd been led to believe. He was a twenty-two-year-old man. A son and father who had worked and been such a help to our family.

The judge listened to our impact statements and said, "I first want to say that I gave the jurors the wrong instructions, so I am throwing out the gun enhancement charge." That was a blow that we'd anticipated because of the judge's earlier statements the first day of the trial.

While waiting for the sentencing, my brother had started a letter-writing campaign, hoping the judge would feel pressured to do the right thing. Over seven thousand letters were sent to the judge. The judge read some of the letters, but he did not like it. He felt the writers had done it all wrong.

The judge went on to declare how he was troubled by the verdict. About the instructions he'd given to the jury causing them to find the defendant guilty of gun enhancement and involuntary manslaughter. That this was not murder, it was involuntary manslaughter. Several times he'd repeat his dismay with the gun enhancement charge. So troubled, he decided to let the attorneys argue about the intentional and unintentional guilty verdict.

The judge would decide the officer's sentencing, and declared this was no more than an accident. He dismissed the gun enhancement charge and said it was necessary for him to throw out the jury verdict. He'd removed the highest charge that could be given for ten years and could now sentence the officer to four years.

I could not believe what the judge said and did. *He was wrong.* Helpless to remain silent, I leapt out of my seat and said, "He's going to throw this trial." He was about to let this killer walk. I could feel in my bones that the judge would do whatever he could to throw the trial and not charge the officer.

Judge Perry rendered his sentence, granting Mehserle with time served for good behavior, and granted him 292 days. He deemed it an accidental shooting, and Johannes Mehserle was sentenced to serve his time for killing Oscar Grant III in county jail. No state prison. He would be out in seven months. His total time spent in jail was eleven months in county jail.

My heart sank. Eleven months in the county jail. If it had been Oscar, it would have been twenty-five to life in prison. I was so disappointed with the judge's new verdict. It was not an accurate representation of what happened to my son. This was not an involuntary manslaughter case, clearly. At the least, he should have been found guilty of voluntary manslaughter. I was hoping for a precise murder charge.

I said then, "My son was murdered, and the law did not hold the killer accountable." I still say the same thing today: *my son was murdered.* My attorney even said this was a miscarriage of justice. The statistics show that Blacks rarely get fair treatment when it involves a police shooting.

I am so reminded of the story of Joseph in the Bible. Joseph went through many things. His brothers were so jealous of him that they sold him into slavery.

Joseph went to prison for doing no wrong. He was later released from jail, and in Genesis 50:20 (KJV), But as for you, ye thought evil against me but God meant it unto good, to bring to pass, as it is this day to save much people alive.

What Satan tried to do was destroy Oscar and me. I believe he tried to kill me, but God used Oscar's tragic death to wake up and start a movement in our society that young men and women are being killed unjustly at the hands of the police. Oscar's death brought me much pain and hurt, but I realize it was for the good. I remember the answer I received in prayer that the Lord had given unto me. I remember the Lord letting me know Oscar and I would be in ministry together. He informed me that Oscar would go through some things in his life. *What kind of things?*

Chapter 17

Money Can Separate Families

While the criminal trial was going on, my attorney for the civil case would fly to Los Angeles to observe and collect facts. During this time, he began planning the strategy for the civil suit.

When dealing with a lawsuit, people have different understandings. One party, known as the plaintiff, files a complaint. In my family's case, we had two attorneys: one for my granddaughter and one for myself.

The dollar amount that families received in California for lawsuits was mostly under three million. However, some families who sued because loved ones were killed at the hands of law enforcement received very low amounts and oftentimes received nothing.

We were seeking twenty-five million dollars in compensation. We knew we would not receive that amount; however, I felt that Oscar's life was worth more than 425 million dollars, so I told my attorney I wanted to sue for the twenty-five million. The process of the suit involved discovery, depositions, past employment, and children. The key to receiving an amount is when families stick together. There are times when families disagree with the amounts being offered and settle separately. This makes it difficult for other family members to continue to pursue their settlement. In my case, my granddaughter's mother settled, so it was no longer necessary for me to continue because I felt that I would not receive more than my granddaughter.

I also know that some mothers do not get any money. This is why it is essential to keep communication open with the victim's wife or fiancée. This way, you will both discuss and decide what you expect and want to happen.

I believed that the lawsuit was not going to be hard to win; it was just a matter of how the case was presented. Having an attorney who will go the extra mile and fight for you trying to get the most available is necessary. It is important because often the attorney asks for thirty-five to forty percent. I felt that because my granddaughter and I both received a settlement, the attorneys made out with more than we received.

I also want to warn that during the lawsuit period there is an opportunity for you to borrow money from the settlement. Take my advice. Don't. Never take money from your settlement before you receive it.

Another key is knowing what the attorneys are talking about and understanding the paperwork presented to you. There are so many different things that you must look at when going through a lawsuit. It's almost as if you have to become an attorney to know what the lawyer is talking about and what actions you should take. And don't allow attorneys to discourage you from pursuing a lawsuit because of past offenses.

Chapter 18
Keeping Oscar's Legacy Alive

After Oscar's death, it was clear to my family that we needed to do something to preserve his legacy. We were in Los Angeles meeting with several people and agreed that Oscar Grant Foundation should be formed.

We started the paperwork that year, but it never got finished. Back in the Bay Area, my brother filled out the paperwork along with our long-time family friend who later became a board member.

Once all the paperwork was submitted, Oscar Grant Foundation was granted 501(c)(3) status in 2010.

Instead of turning to anger and despair, we had chosen love and transformation.

The mission of the Oscar Grant Foundation is to help bridge the gap between young Black men and law enforcement. While nothing can bring Oscar back to his loved ones, we believe it is up to us to create real, meaningful change and fight systemic racism at every level so that all people of color in America —especially Black people – can be safe and thrive."

Creating A Foundation

It takes time to form a foundation:

- solicit the board of directors

- write the by-laws

- write articles of incorporation

- obtain an employer identification number

- apply for a federal tax exempt 501(c)(3) status; California requires state filing.

- register with your state attorney general office

- A few more steps may be required in your state

Costs

There are costs for getting the 501(c)(3) and all the filings. Fees can vary from state to state.

Tax-exempt status, 501(c)(3)

Once the paperwork is complete, the end goal is to become a tax-exempt organization, known as 501(c)(3). Don't get frustrated because it takes time to get your exempt status. It is easy to get the exempt status, but the hard part is following up with all the reporting requirements and ensuring that you stay in compliance.

Some organizations operate without having all their tax status and registrations with the IRS and attorney general office. After learning about the requirements, I found that there are many families that don't have their 501(c)(3) status.

Multiple foundations

After the creation of the two foundations, my brother identified goals and a mission for one organization. Some of the goals of both organizations intersected with one another. Example: both organizations hold weekend retreats. Oscar Grant Foundation caters to women, and the other foundation supports both men and women.

Operating separately makes it difficult when applying for funding. The companies that want to fund the organizations have no idea who the money should be granted to when there are like causes. Families have been hurt and saddened by the splits in organizations formed because of the loss of a loved one. The end goal has to be to keep the loved one's name alive by creating programs that their loved one loved.

To find out more, please go to the following websites:

For more information on creating a foundation in California:

www.irs.gov/charities

www.irs.gov

Keeping Oscar's legacy alive

We do this by offering several programs for the community and police force. The programs have been implemented to make the communities safer. We have five different programs, and each one works towards bridging the gap and helping families improve community relations.

Oscar Grant Foundation Legacy Weekend

I knew I needed to do something for families without resources who were confused about where to turn next. Many other families had suffered the loss of a loved one the way I did. I've written this book about what I've learned on my journey. But, I wanted to come up with something to help them cross over the hurdles as they go through the grieving process. So, I began hosting mothers from across the United States for a weekend getaway, the *Oscar Grant Legacy Weekend.*

I created the event as a way to provide an opportunity to connect with other mothers whose children were murdered by the police or died because of senseless gun violence. The annual event has brought hundreds of mothers from across the country to Oakland.

During the weekend, resource experts teach on different topics. Exercise therapists, mental health experts, attorneys, and local pastors have presented. The idea is to encourage the mothers mentally, spiritually, and emotionally.

So, we always have a comedy performance. The comedian has the women laughing so hard that the tears flow.

We share our stories about our children. On Saturday, we host a gala and have professional singers and entertainers perform.

The galas are grand and crowd pleasers. We pull out all the stops to house the ladies in friendly hotels, pay for their flights to California, and provide food for them. Before the gala, makeup artists and hairstylists groom their hair and apply makeup. It is such a blessing to see these women look so gorgeous. Their happy smiles remind me we're doing the right thing. One year, Tremaine Hawkins came. Yolanda Adams, Major's singer, Darinda Clark-Cole, and so many other artists have been a part of the Legacy Weekend. I cannot name them all. At the events, we have had between 200 to 300 people.

Healing Hurting Hearts (HHH).

We talked about the five stages of grief and it was time for me to do something about it. I formed a support group.

We host our Healing Hurting Hearts program weekly via Zoom and monthly in person at different locations. Families who have lost loved ones to police or community violence are welcome to attend the sessions. Those families who have lost loved ones in other ways are also accepted. During our sessions, we discuss the five grief stages and life after loss. The meetings are designed to give those grieving a chance to heal through different tools, which include devotion, prayer, journaling, music, arts, and exercise. Using the different tools helps individuals learn how to use them to deal with triggers.

Law Enforcement Equity Training

Our Law Enforcement Equity Training focuses on showing the police how to see the humanity in our young Black men more effectively.

Our overall goal is to improve police behavior by showing officers the value in defusing conflicts, identifying mental illness and understanding nonverbal communication, among other things. The end result: police officers have the unique opportunity to be someone's hero, and the youth in our community have their humanity restored.

Academic Enrichment Scholarship Program

Our scholarship program provides funds for students going to college. The students must have a 2.5 grade point average and submit an essay and a recommendation letter from an unrelated professional.

A selection committee reviews the application package, then scores and ranks the applicants.

In 2023, over $40,000 was awarded in scholarships. Our short-term goal is to be able to fund a student from freshman to graduation. We were excited about this goal because we have seen students apply and be selected to attend a prestigious university. Some of the students have graduated and secured full-time employment. The programs we have in place have helped students who live in impoverished neighborhoods.

OG Ballers basketball team

Our OG Ballers basketball teaches students how to get along with one another, share, and have good sportsmanship, which helps the students improve their social skills. Currently, we have four teams that range from ages eight to eighteen.

The teams play at different locations in California and some of the tournaments are played outside of California in Las Vegas, Oregon, Reno and Texas. The older players are taken on HBCU tours of schools available for enrollment. The players learn there is much more to playing basketball than just putting the ball in the basketball hoop. Life skills are taught.

School supply drive

We offer a yearly school supply drive and to date have contributed over 12,250 in backpacks and school supplies. We adopt two schools and provide every student with a choice of backpacks.

Chapter 19

The Movie: Fruitvale Station

Film producer Forest Whitaker called my attorney wanting to talk to me. He wanted to make a film about what happened with Oscar. I gave my attorney permission to share my number. Mr. Whitaker called me and offered his condolences on how sorry he was to see and hear what had happened. He wanted the world to know what happened to Oscar. We talked several times afterwards. He discussed how the film would be made and who the writer would be. Ryan Coogler wrote and made his feature directorial debut, working with Whitaker to complete the film. It was a very low-budgeted production; less than one million dollars was budgeted for the film. During production, the funds were getting low, so actress Octavia Spencer, believing in the film so much, put up money to complete it.

The significance of the true story lies in the twenty-four-hour period of Oscar's life before his death. His beginning the day celebrating my New Year's Eve birthday and later returning with his fiancée and friends from fireworks events in San Francisco.

The film starred Michael B. Jordan portraying Oscar along with Kevin Durand and Chad Michael Murray who both played BART police officers. Octavia Spencer, Melonie Diaz, and Ahna O'Reilly were also cast in starring roles. The making of the movie was very intense with some scenes being filmed on the actual station platform where Oscar was shot by a BART police officer. Before and after filming, often the cast prayed. One day on set with the actors, I was cast in a cameo appearance. I played the daycare provider: I opened the door when the children's parents were dropping them off to daycare.

I spent a lot of time with Octavia Spencer. We went to dinner together and talked for hours to help her gather more information about Oscar and Wanda. She was playing me in the film, so thought it was important to get to know who I am. We talked and laughed; she asked questions. I'm sure this affected her playing the role of his mother better. Her commitment and hard work was lauded after the film opened in several theaters across the country to favorable critic reviews. The film, along with Michael B. Jordan and Octavia Spencer, was nominated and received several awards.

Chapter 20

A Road of Ministry

A memorable speaking opportunity was in Washington, D.C. during one of Rev. Al Sharpton's *Get Your Knee Off My Neck* events. I stood on the same steps where Martin Luther King Jr. stood forty years ago and delivered his *I Have a Dream* speech.

I would address the large crowd numbering ten thousand, if not more. Standing behind the podium, I thought about Dr. King's message and how he must have felt. Did he feel the anxiety then that I felt? I wondered would the audience be receptive to the words that I had penned on my paper.

After a "Good afternoon" greeting, I began telling the crowd that "Lady Liberty is not balanced. There are still some injustices we as a people face." I shared how, because of discrimination, our people are killed at a higher rate.

I shared Micah 6:8. reminding them the verse asks what the Lord requires of you. That you walk justly and walk humbly before God.

I accepted invitations to the White House and to speak in front of many of the country's leaders in Congress and in Sacramento, California at the State Capitol testifying regarding police reform. There were many requests to speak at colleges, universities (Stanford; UTEP, The University of Texas; Bowling Green; Cal State East Bay), and churches to share what happened with Oscar and what was needed to improve our criminal justice system.

I probably would have never met or spoken in front of powerful leaders and students if not for Oscar's blood poured on the concrete. Meeting President Bill and Hillary Clinton, being invited to stand on the stage with Hillary Clinton at the DNC in 2016, dinner with Beyonce and Jay Z, having an opportunity to be in Beyoncé's video, *Lemonade*, and many others. I was cast in a cameo role in a movie, *Fruitvale Station*, which depicts the last twenty-four hours of Oscar's life.

Looking at all the opportunities that I've had, I probably wouldn't be sitting here at 4:16 a.m. on a

Tuesday writing a book about the killing of my son fourteen years ago. Life has a funny way of bringing things to pass. Oscar and I, indeed, are in ministry together, and he is still speaking loud and clear from the grave. I often hear his name on television. Reading an article, a book, or even seeing a picture of him.

Since Oscar's death, I have won many awards for having the perseverance and the determination to seek justice for all. In 2020, I won the MLK Perseverance Award; 2021, the Rizpah Award; and in 2023, the Unstoppable Award.

This is what happens when your pain is turned into purpose and power. You have not gone through what you've gone through for you. The pain is to help others through their journey today. What you've gone through, someone else needs to hear so they can know they are not alone.

Chapter 21
Come On and Fight For Your Child

Origin of *Black Mothers* film

In 2017, I met a young lady named Debora Souza Silva, who was producing a short film about her journey as an activist in the aftermath of Oscar's death. She'd contacted me to request an interview, and I shared about the *Oscar Grant Legacy Weekend*. After the interview, she was convinced that moment in history needed to be documented and I invited her to attend the upcoming event in Oakland.

Although my original intent for the event was creating a means of keeping Oscar's name alive, it quickly grew into so much more. It provided me an opportunity to connect with other mothers whose children were murdered by the police or died because of senseless gun violence. The annual event has brought hundreds of mothers from across the country to Oakland.

The film producer spent the weekend observing my interactions with other mothers. She watched as I walked around the conference room, embracing a group of mothers. Gwen Carr, the mother of Eric Garner; Valerie Bell, the mother of Sean Bell; Lezley Head, the mother of Micheal Brown; and Jeralynn Blueford were among the over two dozen mothers Debora had an opportunity to meet. She would listen intently as we shared familiar stories of personal pain, road-blocking obstacles navigating the judicial system, and even coming toe-to-toe with powerful politicians and police chiefs.

She would often hear—over the years—many of the women describing the gathering as "the sisterhood that was being formed." We would all say no one ever wanted to be a part of it, but that so many Black mothers needed to be in this space for healing. There were so many mothers whose children's names Debora knew from media coverage. But others she didn't recognize because mainstream media often fails to cover those stories.

The media spotlight sensationalizing the brutalization and murders of these women's children has long since faded, but their fight for accountability continues. To fill that *coverage gap*, I've made it part of my mission to share my platform with other mothers. To support and encourage them to keep their children's names alive by telling their stories repeatedly.

It was difficult to hear story after story of personal suffering and loss over that weekend. A reminder to Debora how our injustice system has historically failed our black communities. But most importantly, she also understood that the weekend was filled with love, support, and empowerment. She said she would never forget those moments when she witnessed me comforting, lifting up, and empowering mothers to fight. In my own words, I encouraged mothers "to fight for your child because if you don't, no one else will do it for them." Debora would document: "Wanda Johnson's palpable energy could be felt around the room. As she spoke to the mothers, some of them in tears stood up from their chairs and chanted her words. 'COME ON AND FIGHT!'"

Debora left that gathering determined to tell not only my story ––but the story of a movement of mothers, a movement that I was helping to build out of a lot of pain, mother by mother.

The short film, *Until Something is Done*, eventually aired on PBS and focused on my journey. After the project, Debora could never get that weekend out of her mind. Upon learning about the origin and my crucial role in the coming together of mothers, Debora knew that a film about it needed to be produced. The story of my pursuing justice and building a movement of the mothers demanded to be fully explored through a feature-length documentary.

The Film: *Black Mothers Love & Resist*

From start to finish, the producer Débora Silva spent seven years documenting this powerful movement of mothers and later called the feature film *Black Mothers Love & Resist*.

This is the context in which we situate my film. Activists—including those lead organizers of Black Lives Matter—worked with me and my family as we pressed forward, pursuing accountability for the murder of black people across the city of Oakland, state of California and across the nation. But even before Black Lives Matter became a viral social media hashtag and a global movement, I was already organizing other mothers like myself in churches and hotel conference rooms of Oakland.

Under my mentorship, hundreds of mothers like me from across the country have come to California to build community, learn grassroots organizing strategies, share resources, and gain insight from fellow mothers. California has been a place for restorative retreat, and a political training ground for what we now know as the *mothers of the movement.*

The producer continued her interviews and asked if she could follow me around, shadowing me for five years. My house, my mother's house, and wherever I went, she was there. I remember going to Oscar's gravesite, and she followed me there, asking questions about him, taking photos. During the five years, she would attend OGF events, interviewing me and others.

Debora soon realized it was critical to capture the experience of a mother whose fight for justice was beginning. So, in 2018, she began filming with an Alabama mother—Angela Williams. I met Angela and prayed with her for her son Ulysses Wilkerson, who suffered a beating by Troy police officers. That led to my encouraging and mentoring her. Explaining what she might have to go through when dealing with the court system. Debora intertwined our stories and produced a documentary.

Our stories are familiar, but different. Her son lived and my son died. But, the fact that an injustice had occurred was enough for me to help her fight the system and work to get the justice that her son deserves.

This documentary film shows ways that I mentor other mothers who have lost their loved ones from community and police violence. My support through prayer and the comfort from just being there. The importance of not giving up and fighting for what you believe is right. I have traveled with the documentary to different film festivals throughout the United States.

The film would run on the big screen, and after it was over, I would be a part of the Q&A panel for audience questions. I was one of the protagonists. A protagonist is usually a leading character in a drama, movie, or novel. I would share thoughts and provide an action plan of what the audience could do to help end systemic violence.

I attended the film festival at Martha's Vineyard. A new location for me, I enjoyed touring the beautiful setting. There were so many people there, and something extraordinary happened. I met a businessman from California who owns a theater. He offered to show the film at his place and asked how he might help me and the foundation.

I traveled to Alabama, Texas, Atlanta, New York, San Francisco, Los Angeles, and several other places to showcase the film. We were hoping that someone would purchase the film and show it on the big screen or NETFLIX.

Producer's story

Producer Debora Silva was born outside of the United States, and the topics explored in her films were not foreign to her. She grew up in Brazil, in a predominantly Afro-Brazilian working-class community in São Paulo. She was directly exposed to the realities of racial and social inequality. Throughout her career in journalism, which expanded from Brazil to other countries of the African Diaspora, Debora realized that problems including racial inequality, mass incarceration, and police brutality—ubiquitous amongst communities of color throughout the Americas—are inextricably linked to the legacy of chattel slavery.

Chapter 22

God Has Not Forgotten You

Since the death of Oscar, God has indeed been faithful. From the beginning, He told me Oscar and I would be in ministry. And as I look back, fourteen years have passed and He's shown me Oscar and I in ministry, speaking all over the country. I have been to so many places, only because of Oscar.

A pastor's words spoken over my life regarding my fighting for justice for others has also come to pass. As she'd proclaimed, I'd use my mouth to speak for justice. I have traveled across this country supporting families who have lost loved ones to police violence. Praying and encouraging families, reminding them that God is still in control. I want to share with you as I end this book. Whatever God has promised you concerning your loss, He can and will fulfill the promise.

Romans 8:28 (KJV) says, "And we know that all things work together for good to them that love God, to them who are the called according to his purpose."

Just keep your eyes on Him. Even though you don't see it, God is working on your behalf. God knew before the foundation of the world what would happen to our children or loved ones. We know from reading a previous chapter regarding the stages of grief that God will heal everywhere you hurt. Matthew 5:4 (KJV), Blessed are they that mourn: for they shall be comforted.

God already knew what you and I would endure. He turned that pain into purpose and power. He gave me the strength to stand up for justice and to seek ways to help other families by traveling to where they live and being a support system for them by helping them navigate through the court system.

Oscar's death has forced me to learn so many things I never thought were important to survive. Lawsuits, foundations, strategies to get convictions. You learn to never give up but to keep on pursuing justice and helping others as they go through, to ensure they are not alone.

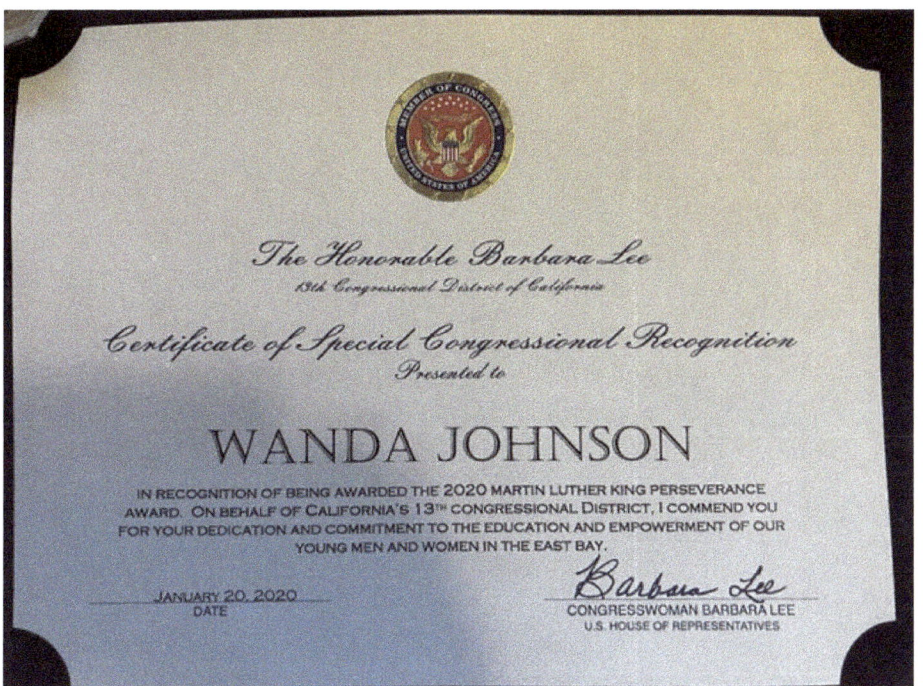

WANDA JOHNSON

FROM TRAGEDY TO TRIUMPH

The Story of Rizpah

2 Samuel 21 8-14 (CEV)

But Saul and Rizpah, the daughter of Aiah had two sons named Armoni and Mephibosheth. Saul's daughter Merab had five sons, whose father was Adriel, the son of Barzillai from Meholah. David took Rizpah's two sons and Merab's five sons. And,

turned them over to the Gibeonites, who hanged all seven of them on the mountain near the place where the Lord was worshiped. This happened right at the beginning of the barley harvest.

Rizpah spread out some sackcloth on a nearby rock. She wouldn't let the birds land on the bodies during the day and kept the wild animals away at night. She stayed there from the beginning of the harvest until it started to rain.

Earlier that Philistines had killed Saul and Jonathan on Mount Gilboa and had hung their bodies in the town square near Beth-Shan.

The people of Jabesh in Gilead had secretly taken the bodies away, but David found out what Saul's wife Rizpah had done, and he went to the leaders of Jabesh to get the bones of Saul and his son Jonathan.

David had their bones taken to the land of Benjamin and buried in a side room in Saul's, family burial place.

Then he gave orders for the bones of the men who had been hanged to be buried there. It was done, and God answered prayers to bless the land.

Wanda's Homemade New Year's Eve Gumbo

INGREDIENTS

- 1 four pack of unsalted butter

- 1 c. All-purpose flour

- 1 small yellow onion, chopped

- 1 medium green bell pepper, chopped (red, green, yellow)

- 6 stalks celery, finely sliced

- 3 green onions

- 4 packages of andouille sausage, sliced into 1/2" rounds

- Cajun seasoning

- Kosher salt

- Seasoned salt

- Garlic powder and Garlic salt

- Freshly ground black pepper

- 16 c. chicken broth

- 2 Roasted whole chickens cooked separately

- 1 bay leaf

- 3 bags of medium shrimp, peeled, deveined,

- 6 Crabs cleaned

- 2 bags of white rice for serving

DIRECTIONS

Step 1 In a large, deep skillet over medium-low heat, melt butter, then add flour. Cook, stirring constantly, until roux is dark colored, 12 to 15 minutes.

Step 2 Add celery, bell pepper (red, green, and yellow), and both onions, stirring until softened. Then add a pinch of the following seasonings to taste: seasoned salt, salt, black pepper, cajun seasoning, garlic salt, garlic powder and cook, stirring, until softened, about 8 minutes.

Step 3 Cook sausage separately and strain the grease once sausage is fully cooked.

Step 4 Stir in sausage, crab, cut up chicken into mixture with broth, and bay leaf and bring to a boil. Reduce heat to low and simmer, stirring occasionally, until thickened, about 1 hour.

Step 5 In the last 4 minutes of cooking, add shrimp. Once the shrimp is pink and cooked through, taste and adjust the seasonings. Do not overcook shrimp too long.

Step 6 Cook rice for 20 minutes and strain.

Remove Gumbo from heat and serve over white rice.

This was Oscar's favorite dish every year for New Year's Eve. We had family dinner and ate Gumbo.

About the Author

Rev. Wanda Johnson is the Executive Director of the Oscar Grant Foundation. She serves at Landmark Restoration Christian Fellowship as Associate Pastor under the direction of Pastor Kimberly Heidelberg. She is a first-time author and #1 Amazon Best Seller. Wanda Johnson has co-authored an anthology, *Her Unbreakable Spirit,* released December 2023.

Wanda's voice resonates as a magnified embodiment of compassion, fiercely dedicated to the pursuit of justice. Her mission is to help others learn to forgive themselves through prayer, grief sessions, and support groups.

As a certified peer specialist at the National Alliance on Mental Illness in Contra Costa County, Wanda's dedication is tangible, offering a lifeline of understanding.

Her academic pursuits, including a bachelor's in business management and a master's degree in human resource management from Golden Gate University, mirror her commitment to growth. Currently enrolled in the Nonprofit Certification Program at Cal State East Bay.

Philippians 4:13 (KJV). I can do all things through Christ, which strengthened me.

Connect with Wanda

- Website: https://oscargrantfoundation.org

- Website: https://herunbreakablespirit.com/

- Website: Wandajohnsonspeaks.com

- Facebook: Wanda Johnson

Instagram: rev_wanda_johnson

www.ingramcontent.com/pod-product-compliance
Lightning Source LLC
Chambersburg PA
CBHW060820190426
43197CB00038B/2169